The Dutch East India Company and Britisl
History and Legacy of the World's Most Fam

By Charles River Ed

A depiction of VOC ships

About Charles River Editors

Charles River Editors is a boutique digital publishing company, specializing in bringing history back to life with educational and engaging books on a wide range of topics. Keep up to date with our new and free offerings with this 5 second sign up on our weekly mailing list, and visit Our Kindle Author Page to see other recently published Kindle titles.

We make these books for you and always want to know our readers' opinions, so we encourage you to leave reviews and look forward to publishing new and exciting titles each week.

Introduction

The Dutch India Company

An 18th century depiction of the company's shipyard

"Whereas pepper has nothing in it that can plead as a recommendation to fruit or berry, its only desirable quality being a certain pungency; and yet it is for this that we import it all the way from India!" – Pliny the Elder

From classic grilled meat to exotic and savory 5-star dishes, pepper has long been the ultimate staple spice. While bulk pepper may be readily stocked in supermarkets and convenience stores today, there was once a time when the common spice was considered one of the most valuable commodities in the world. Merchants tripped over one another to get their hands on the tiny black beads, which live in colorful clusters of berry-like shells reminiscent of Christmas lights. They were so precious that an uncountable number of men crossed the turbulent and uncharted seas for them. In fact, the tropical spice was so highly sought after that blood was shed over the edible gold.

To many, the mention of maritime merchants evokes an imagery of growling pirates donned in their stereotypical hats and a colorful parrot perched upon their shoulders. These nautical rascals wander the high seas in search of treasure and adventure. Though that imagery may be inaccurate, the real life companies that once dominated international waters operated on a similar thirst for conquest and riches.

Perhaps the most famous – or as many would put it, infamous – of these naval corporations was the Dutch East India Company, also known as VOC. Established around the beginning of the 17th century, this nautical behemoth of a corporation was determined to squeeze everyone else out of the market. Vested with the power to wage war and exterminate any who dared stand in their way, the rest of the world stood by as the unstoppable force took over the whole of international maritime trade. The company would crush its opponents on the way to the top, establishing a monopoly on the global spice trade that would not only rock the world but forever change the course of modern business history.

The British East India Company

The East India Company's flag

"With regard, therefore, to the abuse of the external federal trust, I engage myself to you to make good these three positions. First, I say, that from Mount Imaus (or whatever else you call that large range of mountains that walls the northern frontier of India), where it touches us in the latitude of twenty-nine, to Cape Comorin, in the latitude of eight, that there is not a single prince, state, or potentate, great or small, in India, with whom they have come into contact, whom they have not sold: I say sold, though sometimes they have not been able to deliver according to their bargain. Secondly, I say, that there is not a single treaty they have ever made which they have not broken. Thirdly, I say, that there is not a single prince or state, who ever put any trust in the Company, who is not utterly ruined; and that none are in any degree secure or flourishing, but in the exact proportion to their settled distrust and irreconcilable enmity to this nation." - Edmund Burke, 1783

The British East India Company served as one of the key players in the formation of the British Empire. From its origins as a trading company struggling to keep up with its superior Dutch, Portuguese, and Spanish competitors to its tenure as the ruling authority of the Indian subcontinent to its eventual hubristic downfall, the East India Company serves as a lens through which to explore the much larger economic and social forces that shaped the formation of a global British Empire. As a private company that became a non-state global power in its own right, the East India Company also serves as a cautionary tale all too relevant to the modern world's current political and economic situation.

On its most basic level, the East India Company played an essential part in the development of long-distance trade between Britain and Asia. The trade in textiles, ceramics, tea, and other goods brought a huge influx of capital into the British economy. This not only fueled the Industrial Revolution, but also created a demand for luxury items amongst the middle classes. The economic growth provided by the East India Company was one factor in Britain's ascendancy from a middling regional power to the most powerful nation on the planet. The profits generated by the East India Company also created incentive for other European powers to follow its lead, which led to three centuries of competition for colonies around the world. This process went well beyond Asia to affect most of the planet, including Africa and the Middle East.

Beyond its obvious influence in areas like trade and commerce, the East India Company also served as a point of cultural contact between Western Europeans, South Asians, and East Asians. Quintessentially British practices such as tea drinking were made possible by East India Company trade. The products and cultural practices traveling back and forth on East India Company ships from one continent to another also reconfigured the way societies around the globe viewed sexuality, gender, class, and labor. On a much darker level, the East India Company fueled white supremacy and European concepts of Orientalism (See Said, Orientalism).

In the same vein, as a joint stock company, the East India Company left behind meticulous documentation of its economic exchanges and policies. Descriptions of military endeavors, encounters with indigenous peoples, and codes of conduct for employees also give contemporary researchers insight into the cultural perspectives of those who governed the company. Moreover, the East India Company's policies and personnel were the subject of frequent commentaries in newspapers, parliamentary debates, and other publicly available sources. Historians have used these detailed records to reconstruct both the day-to-day operations and the larger historical arc of the company. In addition, the sources created by the East India Company provide insight into the far less well-documented histories of the people the East India Company encountered, traded with, and ultimately conquered.

One of the major reasons that the East India Company remains the subject of intense interest is that the consequences of its influence remain visible in India, Britain, and other parts of the world to this day. While the British Crown eventually replaced the East India Company as the governing authority of India, the systems of production they had established remained intact. More than half a century after India declared independence from the British Empire, the economic and cultural effects of this colonial system of production remained apparent. The disparities in wealth and power between the Global North and the Global South may not stem from the East India Company alone, but the company played an indisputable role in imperial processes.

The Dutch East India Company and British East India Company: The History and Legacy of the World's Most Famous Colonial Trade Companies examines how the rabid consumer craving of a particular spice jumpstarted the legendary corporation, and how the Dutch East India Company rose to prominence through a brutal mix of financial acumen, merciless violence, and highly controversial business tactics. Along with pictures of important people, places, and events, you will learn about the Dutch East India Company and British East India Company like never before.

The Dutch East India Company and British East India Company: The History and Legacy of the World's Most Famous Colonial Trade Companies

The Dutch East India Company

The Dutch Miracle

"Every man thus lives by exchanging, or becomes in some measure a merchant, and the society itself grows to be what is properly a commercial society." – Adam Smith

The earliest use of pepper dates back to 3000 BC in India, with some archaeologists pushing the date even further back. South Indians are believed to have been jazzing up their dishes with the seasoning since the Stone Age. Evidence from 1300 BC also hints at a trade relationship of sorts between India and Egypt. Peppercorns were found lodged in the nostrils of mummified pharaoh, Ramses the Great. This is yet another clue of how sacred the spice truly was in ancient civilization.

By the first century, the Romans had gotten into the blossoming international trade. Merchant vessels from the ports of Rome braved the rough seas to the southwestern coast of India. Shiploads of Roman-minted silver and gold were swapped for Indian cloves, cinnamon, sandalwood, diamonds, pearls, rubies – and of course, pepper. The foreign spices were a huge hit in Alexandria, the trading hub of Rome. Pepper, along with other Asian spices and herbs, were used for medicinal purposes, such as disinfectant poultice creams and drinking syrups. The extract from the versatile spice was also found in balms and perfumed oils used for slathering around the neck and under the arms after baths.

Neighboring nations began to hone in on the spice and were anxious to dip their beaks into the growing trading pool. In 410, an army dispatched by the Visigoths, an ancient Germanic people, invaded Rome. To keep the invaders from destroying the city, Romans agreed to cough up vast quantities of gold, silver, silk, animal skins, and 3,000 pounds of pepper. The sum would not keep the Visigoths happy for long, as they went ahead and took control of the city, anyway. This was known as the "Sack of Rome."

While imperial Rome crumbled, other nations swiftly swooped in on the gap in the market. Arab traders from the Middle East and Africa became the biggest players of the international spice game. Eager to keep their upper hand, they drove the price of pepper up and spread rumors to ward off their competition. Pepper-crazy explorers were warned that the plants, which were located in Indian groves and the Caucus Mountains, were "guarded" by swarms of lethal, poison-spitting serpents.

Arab traders were soon forced to share the spice trade with the influx of nations venturing out to sea. By the Middle Ages, pepper and other rare Asian spices had become associated with the European upper class, and as their popularity grew, it became a form of currency. Based on a German price table circa 1393, a pound of ginger could be exchanged for a sheep. A pound of saffron was about as valuable as a strong, healthy horse. Of all the spices, pepper was most commonly used for monetary exchange.

It cost Europeans and other foreigners a hefty 10 pounds of pepper up front just to trade with English merchants. Due to the coin shortage, taxes, tolls, and fines could be settled by peppercorn kernels. Instead of jewelry, china, or fine clothing, brides-to-be received pepper plants as dowry. Some tenants even paid their landlords with "peppercorn rent."

By the end of the 13th century, Venetian merchant traveler Marco Polo jotted down the fascinating ways foreigners across the world used their spices. Afghans drank delicious wines fermented from wines and a variety of spices, and seasoned their meat with salt and pepper. In Hangzhou, China, 10,000-lbs of pepper were brought into the city on the daily. Many believe it was Polo's memoirs that intensified the European interest in the spice trade.

A medieval depiction of Marco Polo

As time progressed, the reins of the spice trade would be repeatedly snatched by numerous hands around the globe. By the 14th century, those hands belonged to Genoa, a city in northwest Italy. Once again, pepper became the most widely traded commodity in the up-and-coming trading hub. By the end of the 15th century, over 400 tons of pepper was being imported into the neighboring city of Venice. Venetian pepper merchants made their profits by marking up the price of pepper by 40%.

Genoa-born explorer Christopher Columbus was another who recorded his observations on foreign spice use. During his second voyage in 1493, a scientist named Diego Chanca tagged along, and together, they discovered red pepper and allspice, which they brought back and shared with Spain.

A posthumous portrait of Columbus

By the 1500s, Portugal had become another prevalent player in the field. Just a few years before the start of the 16th century, Vasco da Gama was tasked with establishing a trade route to India, where he was to search for "Christian and spices." Though 30% of Portuguese shipping vessels never returned, Portugal dominated the spice trade throughout the 16th century. Every year, 2 million kilograms of pepper, cinnamon, ginger, and nutmeg teemed into Lisbon. The risky voyages saw a substantial tax placed on cargoes of East Indian vessels. Middlemen traders also tacked premiums onto the price of spices.

Vasco da Gama

As the 16th century came to a close, however, the reins of the spice trade slipped yet again from the hands of the Portuguese. In the late 16th century and onward, the provinces of Northern Netherlands entered what historians refer to as the "Dutch Miracle." No one was prepared for the plain cousins of then-bustling Southern Netherlands to forge ahead of the spice race, and yet the Dutch Golden Age soon fell in place thanks to a number of reasons.

To understand what led to the Dutch's sudden prominence, one must travel back to 1568. Before the mid-1500s, the territories known as Belgium and Holland today were composed of 17 lowland provinces belonging to Burgundy. These lands came under the control of Charles V, King of Spain and Holy Roman Emperor, in 1506. In 1568, his son, Philip II, intervened in said territories once more to quell the movement of the Protestant Reformation, but disgruntled dwellers in the 5 northern provinces did not take kindly to this and revolted against the king. 11 years later, 7 of the provinces officially declared their independence with the Union of Utrecht. From then on, they dubbed themselves the United Provinces. Just 6 years later, the Siege of Antwerp of 1585 drew a dashed line between Northern and Southern Netherlands, formally dividing the regions.

Charles V

Philip II

Before the siege, the city of Antwerp was the leading center of commerce in all of Europe. Antwerp welcomed Catholic and Protestant merchants alike, and it was this unbiased attitude that propelled them to the top of the ladder. Merchants from Germany, England, and the new United Provinces all flocked to Antwerp to trade an assortment of goods, including grains, Baltic timber, and exquisite Dutch textiles. One of the commodities Dutch merchants readily accepted was Iberian salt, which was used in preserving herring and other Dutch delicacies.

The decision made by Alexander Farnese, the Duke of Parma, to invade Antwerp came with lasting consequences. Going against the tradition of ruling Catholic powers of the time, Farnese allowed Protestants to evacuate the city peacefully. At the same time, Philip II, Farnese's uncle, imposed a ban on trade against the United Provinces and confiscated all trading ships from the ports of Spain and Portugal. The king had unwittingly created a population of roaming Antwerp Protestants, the majority of which were skilled craftsmen, seamen, and wealthy merchants. Backed by years and experience of international trade, they would soon take the industry by storm.

Farnese

Most Protestant refugees made their new homes in the city of Amsterdam. The population in the capital of Holland, then an obscure trading port, ballooned from 30,000 residents to 105,000. The multicultural community of Amsterdam had quickly become one of the most highly populated cities in all of Europe.

From then on marked a glowing period of religious, scientific, technological, and artistic advancements in Holland. The world was introduced to the creative genius of Rembrandt and Pieter Hooft, as well as the likes of Christiaan Huygens, who invented the pendulum clock. In the late 16th century, Holland decided that they, too, wanted in on the spice trade.

In 1591, the Portuguese established a syndicate between German, Italian and Spanish firms, utilizing Hamburg as its central port. This syndicate essentially excluded the Dutch from nautical trade. Infuriated Dutch merchants vowed to find a way into the industry themselves, beginning with their observations as the Portuguese trading system fell apart. To start off, the syndicate could not match the increasing demands of certain commodities, especially pepper, and each time the syndicate failed to meet the supply quota for pepper, the spice saw a dramatic increase in prices. The Dutch finally found their way in when a couple of traveling merchants, Cornelius de Houtman and Jan Huyghen van Linschoten, allegedly gained access to confidential Portuguese trade routes and learned their business practices.

A portrait of van Linschoten

Van Linschoten, who was formerly based in the Indian city of Goa as a secretary to the Portuguese archbishop, headed home to Holland in 1592. Inspired by the rich culture and bountiful resources in Southeast Asia, he took pen to paper and wrote a recollection of his experiences. The book, entitled *Itinerario*, offered descriptions of the picturesque landscape, as well as insight into navigation and potential trade routes. A small compilation of detailed maps were also included in the book, featuring the works of cartographers such as brothers Arnoldus and Henricus van Langren. Van Linschoten wrote, "In this place of Sunda, there is much pepper, and it is better than that of India or Malabar... It hath likewise much frankinscence, camphor, and diamonds, to which men might very well traffic without much impeachment, for that the Portugals come not thither..."

Simply put, Dutch voyagers were instructed to sail south of Sumatra, a Western Indonesian island, then north of the Sunda Strait, which lay between Java and Sumatra. This, van Linschoten insisted, was the only way to skirt around the Portuguese ships. The *Itinerario* sold like umbrellas on a pouring day, with translated versions popping up in England, France, and Germany. Likewise, those in his home country took the navigational advice to heart.

The Rise of the VOC

"So long as Holland has been Holland, such richly laden ships have never been seen." – Unknown

In 1594, Reiner Pauw, Jean Corel, and Dirk van Os, along with a small group of merchants hailing from Antwerp and Amsterdam, established a syndicate of their own. They called their new company the "Compagnie van Verre" – the Company of Far Lands. The next year, the CFL sent 249 sailors, spread over 4 ships, to India on a quest for spices and other blue-chip items.

This expedition took the ships to Banten, a province in the Java island of Indonesia. The ideal location was also a major pepper port. There, Dutch crewmen were fended off by both indigenous natives angered by the unannounced trip and Portuguese merchants who had previously claimed the land. The Dutch crew moved along to the northern coast of the island, but they were only greeted with more conflict. An ambush by Javanese locals resulted in the casualties of 12 Dutch crewmen and a Javanese prince at Madura.

After 3 years of rough seas and the mini-battles that ensued abroad, only 89 Dutch crewmen made their way back to Holland. On top of their obvious lack of planning and shoddy organizational skills, the ships returned with only a single cargo of pepper, and little to no other spices or valuable goods. Nevertheless, even with the seemingly unimpressive haul, merchants were still able to make a tidy profit.

The phenomenon excited other wealthy Dutch merchants, who found a fresh opportunity and pounced on it. That same year, in 1597, Vincent van Bronkhorst, Cornelius van Campen, and another band of Dutch merchants formed a company of their own. They called it the "Nieuwe Compagnie te Amsterdam (New Company of Amsterdam)." By 1599, 6 new companies from Rotterdam, Delft, and Zeeland, all motivated by the same agenda, had come to fruition.

Among these companies was one founded by a reputable merchant, Isaac Le Maire. Le Maire joined forces with merchants from different Dutch cities, including Louis de la Beeque and Jacques de Velaer, and founded the Nieuwe Brabantse Compagnie. Later that year, Amsterdam's burgomasters (mayor-like officials) gifted the NBC a charter for trade with China. The following year, NBC was permitted to partner up with Expert Compagnie, forming the newly united Veriniqde Compagnie te Amsterdam (the United Amsterdam Company). 8 massive ships fit to fight the most passionate of waters were added to the merged company's assets, which were to be commanded by Captain Jacob van Neck.

Qui fœta lustravit Batavis incognita Nautis,
et non visa priùs per Gallos, atque Britannos,
ac Lusitanós Indorum nomine claros,
Christicolasvè alios, sulcantis æquora velis,
sic sua Jacobus Lemarius ora ferebat.

Le Maire

Van Neck

Once again, the Dutch companies sent a combined fleet of at least 22 ships to the East. As expected, only 14 of these vessels made it back home, with over half of the crew either lost at sea or in battle. But this time, the cargo featured a whopping 600,000 pounds of pepper and other rare spices, earning Dutch merchants an even handsomer profit.

In late 1600, van Neck's ships produced results that put a sparkling grin on the faces of Dutch merchants everywhere. His successful voyage became the first to touch bases with the "Spice Islands" of Maluku. This eliminated the need for Javanese middlemen, and in turn, Dutch merchants raked in a 400% profit. It was then that the Dutch knew they were truly in business.

At that point, it was high time for retaliation. In the spirit of the Portuguese syndicate, the Dutch companies realized that unity would be the key to driving the Portuguese out of the spice industry. In the last weeks of 1600, the Dutch collaborated with Muslim merchants on the Ambon Island of Indonesia. Their agreement entailed that the Dutch be granted exclusive rights to the purchasing of all spices on the island.

Traditionally, European maritime companies operated under one similar and increasingly dated system. Unlike modern corporations today, an entire company would be established for the purpose of a single round trip voyage to the East Indies. Once what was left of the ships returned, the company disintegrated. The defunct company then distributed profits between shareholders, and proceeded to either sell or auction off their inventory and equipment. Conversely, the new Dutch establishments set out to change the antiquated system, breathing "semi-permanent life" into their companies. While most companies were formed to take on just one voyage, the Dutch were granted a single charter that allowed them to oversee a series of them. This meant that rather than having a constant rotation of control, the same set of directors and board members were kept on staff throughout the voyages. Finally, when the voyages were deemed complete, the same directors would take the profit and capital from the now buried companies to start a brand new one.

In 1601, the Dutch were on a mission to quench their spice cravings. 6 of these companies released 65 ships on 14 voyages to the Cape of Good Hope, the rocky border in the Cape Peninsula of South Africa. The scramble for spices took a definitive toll on the nation's trade. While bidding prices in Indonesia soared, merchants in Amsterdam were forced to lower their prices as local competition began to heat up.

Profits were at an all-time low. The Dutch government, which felt its power dwindling, knew the problem had to be remedied, and fast. If the Dutch did not act now, the swelling unified powers of Portugal and Spain would push them out of the industry altogether, rendering all their accomplishments thus far completely useless. Meanwhile, a more ominous threat loomed over the Dutch market, as the English were already one step ahead of them. Just a year before, English seafaring companies combined their powers in one of the world's earliest monopoly enterprises: the British East India Company.

On March 20, 1602, the Dutch followed by example, marking another page in history. The 6 rival companies – the United Amsterdam Company, the Veerse Compagnie, the Verenigde Zeeuwse Compagnie, the Magellaanse Rotterdamse Compagnie, the Moucheron van der Hagen & Compagnie, the Een andere Rotterdamse Compagnie, and the Delftse Vennooteschappe Compagnie – combined their powers into a single entity. The new "mega-merger" of a corporation became known as Vereenigde Oostindische Compagnie – formally referred to as the United Dutch Chartered East India Company. Traders from the nearby cities of Enkhuizen and Hoorn were also invited to the trade of the newly-formed cartel.

With blessings from the Dutch government and a starting capital of approximately 6,440,200 guilders (roughly $644 million in USD today), the VOC could now reign as a monopoly over all Asian trade. The charter bestowed upon the company the right to build and maintain armies, erect forts overseas, and the power to handle treaties with Asian rulers however they saw fit. This charter, which would be valid for 21 years, also suggested that board members perform a routine audit every 10 years.

A picture of the VOC's headquarters from the Amsterdam Municipal Department for the Preservation and Restoration of Historic Buildings and Sites

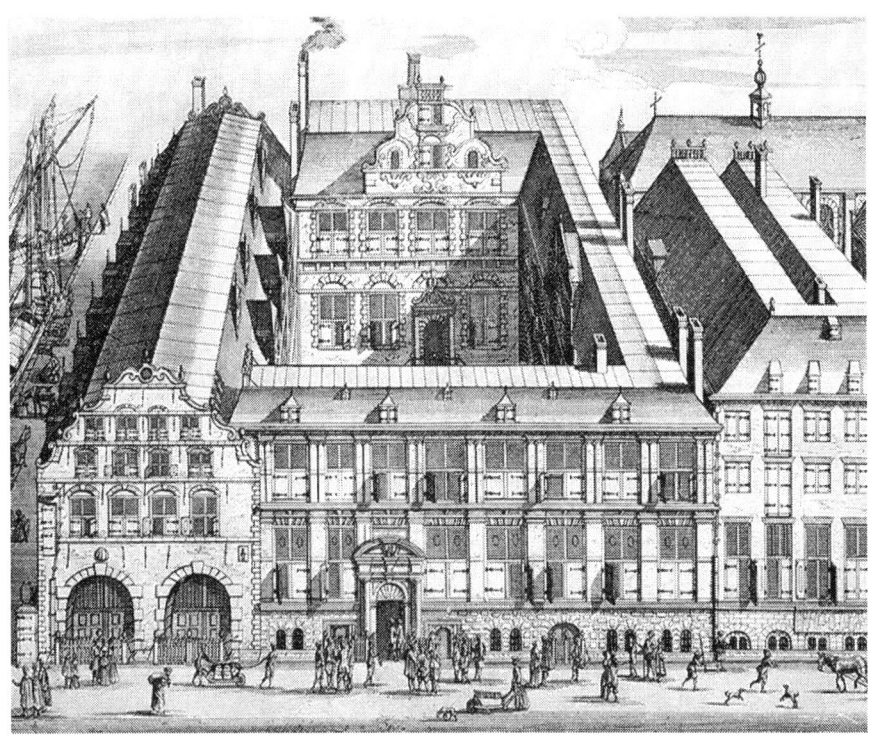

An 18th century sketch of the headquarters

Proud members of the Dutch super-corporation flaunted their new flags in front of their VOC chambers. These company flags, rippling in the morning breeze, featured the company's logo stitched onto a background of Dutch colors – which was then orange, white, and blue. The VOC logo was as notoriously recognizable as it was simple – a large V in the center, with a shrunken "O" and "C" on each leg of the letter. The first initial of the chamber's location was added to the crown of the logo for each respective base. These logos would soon be stamped upon all VOC items – from the sides of shipping vessels, to products, and onto the faces of coins minted by the company themselves.

The company's logo

A VOC monogram once positioned above the entrance to the Cape of Good Hope

The VOC, which is now considered the world's first limited liability company, chose to modernize their business practices. Merchants were now allowed to pour their money into hundreds of ships from the VOC sub-companies at one time. This was especially enticing, as this minimized risk meant that if one of the ships they invested in never made it back, they would not be left in financial ruin. Even more appealing, lucky merchants who saw most of their ships return obtained separate sums of profit from every vessel they had invested in.

The VOC would not only issue the world's first IPO (initial public offering), which allowed public access to the private company's stocks, the company is also credited with creating the stock market. The VOC capital was split into shares worth 3,000 guilders each (roughly $300,000 USD today), and the shares were sold on the Amsterdam Stock Exchange, another brainchild of the VOC. The sale of stocks raised the capital needed to construct a top-of-the-line fleet of ships that would make their competitors' vessels pale in comparison. The rest of the bonds, or debt investments, were then set aside to fund each voyage of the VOC.

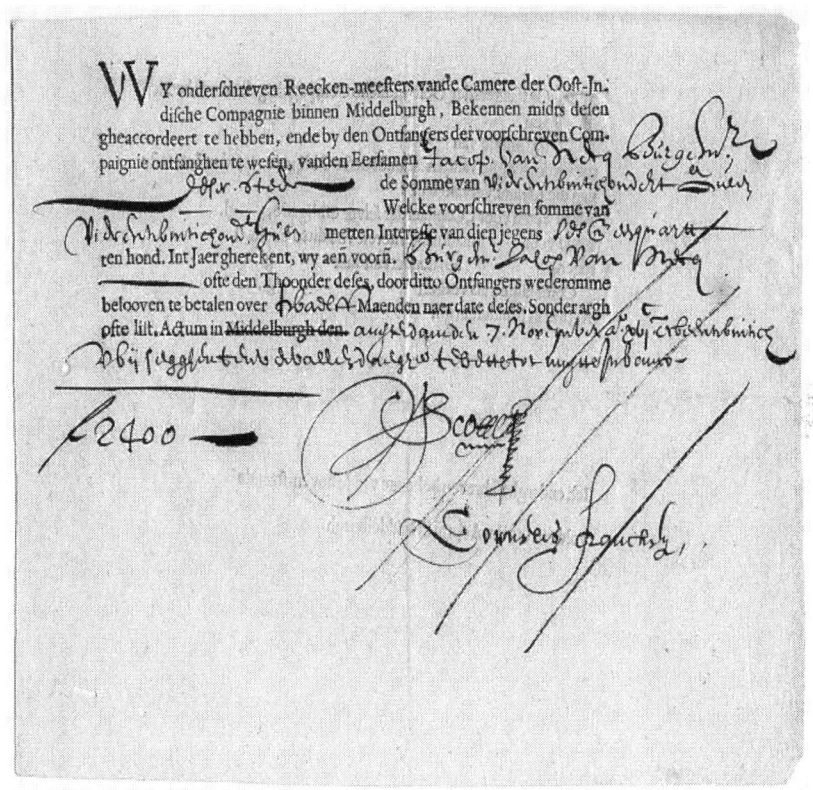

A bond issued by the company in 1623

In the same vein, the VOC would also produce its own form of currency. They minted their own coins stamped with the VOC logo in gold, silver, bronze, and sometimes, pewter. Minting factories dedicated to producing the coins were set up in the Netherlands and in Asia. Throughout the years of the VOC's existence, the company's currencies – guilders, ducatoons, and stivers – were used in all trade and barter.

A coin minted by the VOC

While pre-VOC companies were manned by a loose group of management with no clear boundaries of power between directors and regular staff, members and shareholders of the VOC were distinguished by 2 groups. There were the participanten, or the general, non-managing population of the corporation. The latter were known as the bewindhebbers, a group of 60-76 directors that oversaw all VOC operations. Those who were looking to liquidate their interests in the limited liability company could only pawn them off at the single-stock exchange. Issac Le Maire of former UAC fame was the VOC's largest shareholder.

6 main chambers, which were situated in Rotterdam, Delft, Hoorn, Middelburg, Enkhuizen, and Amsterdam, made up the VOC. Bewindhebber shareholders were selected to represent each chamber as a single board of directors known as the "Heeren XVII," – the Lords Seventeen. The Amsterdam chamber, with 8 delegates, was the most influential, and therefore held the decisive vote pertaining to all internal disagreements and disputes.

The Heeren XVII held 2 to 3 meetings annually, each of which would last up to 3-4 weeks at a time. A variety of matters would be covered in these meetings. Delegates pitched ideas about their next purchases in Asia, as well as methods to solidify those deals. They organized the construction of new trading vessels and designed the roster of crew members and equipment on their ships. Those who were looking to travel to Asia themselves could announce their plans for visit and obtain resources and accompaniment from the VOC if needed. Unruly and drunken behavior of company members during staff parties and gatherings were also discussed, and the offending parties subsequently reprimanded.

One of the new advantages the VOC enjoyed came in the form of shrunken interest rates. Dutch businesses were now allowed to obtain loans at a 4% interest rate. This was a paltry figure in comparison to the more than double 10% rate English businesses had to abide by. This also meant that the VOC could now invest in more than twice the number of ships, equipment, and labor than its English counterpart.

Although the VOC had, in a sense, piggybacked on the ideas of the British East India Company, the modified system set in place would soon see them leap ahead of their main competition. Coupled with what historians have described as financial acumen way beyond their years, and their possession of untouchable self-governing powers, the VOC was now fully equipped to blow everyone else out of the water. No one would see them coming until it was too late.

The Quest for Asia and the First Alliance

A depiction of VOC uniforms

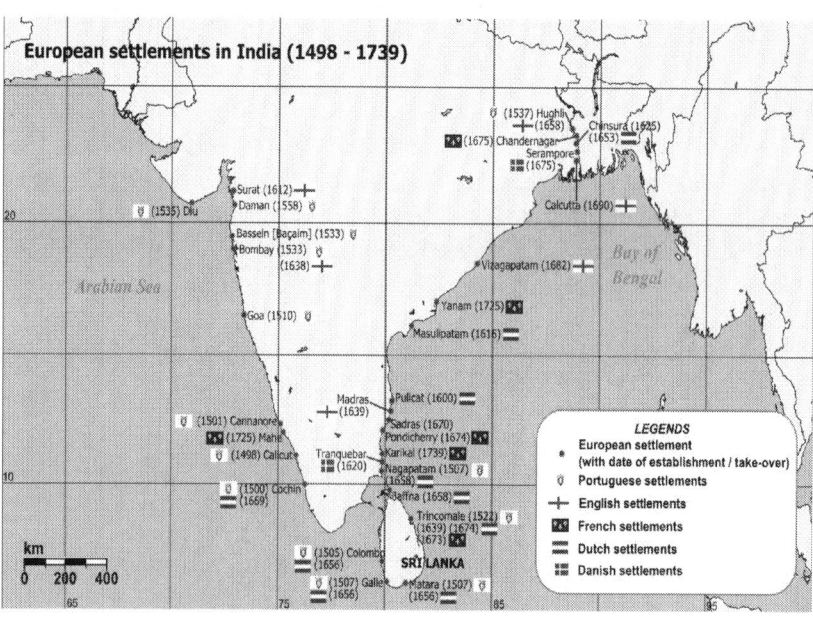

A map of various settlements in the region

"Be not astonished at new ideas; for it is well known to you that a thing does not therefore cease to be true because it is not accepted by many." – Baruch Spinoza, Dutch philosopher

The year that followed the founding of the VOC was nothing short of action-packed. In the beginning of 1603, the company revisited Banten in the Java islands. There, they officially established their first permanent trading post.

Around the same time, on the 25th of February, a fleet of Dutch ships surrounded a Portuguese vessel named the *Santa Catarina*. Outnumbered, the gleaming 1,500-ton ship surrendered to the VOC ships 10 hours into the attack. The daytime battle resulted in the deaths of at least 70 crewmen. The Dutch ships then proceeded to swipe the treasure trove of Chinese spices, clothes, and textiles on board before making the trip back home. Much to the merchants' delight, the stolen loot was estimated to be worth over 3 million guilders. Not only did this bring a 50% increase in capital to the VOC, the company was now worth 5 times more than the British East India Company.

The seizure of the *Santa Catarina* was said to have been orchestrated by the VOC and the Johoreans, natives from a Southern Malaysian state. It was this event that began an amicable relationship between the VOC and Johorean leaders, one that would last well into the 18th century. Moreover, this event would soon prove historically significant for other reasons.

The wildly successful auction of the *Santa Catarina* booty boggled the minds of merchants from other European nations. Before this, the Portuguese, who had a head-start in the industry, had managed to keep their trade relations with Asian ports under wraps. Now that the secret was out, the potential of the vast and unimaginable riches available in Asia – in particular, China – stunned merchants across Europe, which only amped up the competition for the VOC.

The *Santa Catarina* incident was also the source of one of the company's first brushes with controversy. Admiral Jacob van Heemskerk, the commander of the batch of invading ships, came under fire; since his ships had not been formally sanctioned as a privateer (private soldiers or ships that engaged in maritime warfare in exchange for commissions), critics condemned his actions as "an act of piracy."The new criticism prompted the VOC to hire one of the earliest versions of a corporation publicist. They sought the help of Hugo Grotius, a lawyer and scholar of the Dutch Renaissance, and tasked him with drawing up a quick pamphlet that would both defend and justify the VOC's actions.

Jacob van Heemskerk

Grotius

Grotius' subsequent publication, *Mare Liberum*, published in 1609, went a step further than that. His book, which translates to "The Freedom of the Seas," was directed towards the Portuguese and their attempt at monopolizing trade in the East Indies. The commentary illustrated the idea that the "limitless" seas were international territory and therefore public domain, meaning no nation could claim ownership of it. He asserted, "Every nation is free to travel to every other nation, and to trade with it."

Furthermore, Grotius was adamant that the VOC ships had engaged in a "just war." As the Portuguese themselves were the first to use "unlawful force" to ensure their hold on the Asian trade market, the VOC was supposedly "defending the freedom" of Euro-Asian navigation. His work is often said to have laid down the foundations for moral law and international business ethics.

Following the *Santa Catarina* incident, a Portuguese naval commander, Estevao Teixeira de Macedo, gnashed his teeth at the Johoreans. Enraged by the Johoreans alliance with the VOC and the role they played in capturing the Santa Catarina, de Macedo sent aggressive ships and galleons – massive, armed cargo vessels with multiple decks – to the Johor River. There, de

Macedo's men beleaguered the locals who resided along or near the coastline. A barricade was also set up to prevent goods from flowing in and out of the region, and to prevent history from repeating itself.

In early October of 1603, 4 VOC ships would be directly involved in a chain of skirmishes that took place along the Singapore Straits and Johor River. These incidents are collectively known as the Battle of Changi. The ships, which were governed by Admiral Wijbrand van Warwijk and his second-in-command, Vice Admiral Jacob Pietersz van Enkhuysen, reached the Johor shores. Once again, they successfully made contact with local fishermen and befriended the Johorean royal court. Hearing about the new blockades imposed upon the Johoreans, the VOC agreed to team up with them once more to put a stop to the Portuguese for good.

On the 10th of October, the VOC ships skulked up to the river bound for Johor, where they had first stumbled upon the Portuguese ships 8 months ago. The fog thinned, revealing the *Todos os Santos*, the target flagship with the most high-ranking officials on board. With the enemy vessel in clear view, the Dutch ships attacked. They loaded up their cannons and fired into the sails of the galleon. With gaping holes bored through the blazing sails, the Portuguese ship came to a full stop, stupefied by the unheralded attack. What was left of the Portuguese crew staggered out to the main deck and hastily lowered their emergency getaway boats. Some were able to paddle away to temporary safety. They caught up with each other in the secluded shallow waters of Batam, another Indonesian island. After sticking it out for another day, the Portuguese crewmen surrendered in the wee hours of October 11.

Bolstered by the string of victories, the VOC decided it was time to think bigger. Just 2 months later, on the 18th of December, Admiral Steve van der Hagen, a seasoned captain and mobile merchant, was put in charge of the company's first official fleet. The fleet consisted of 13 vessels outfitted with premium-quality naval artillery and a specially trained crew of 1,200 men. The meticulously crafted Dutch ships, which were smaller than average, were not only faster, but was made for easy navigation – ideal for naval warfare.

STEVEN van der HAGEN.

Admiral Steve van der Hagen

Under explicit VOC instructions, the admiral was to reinforce attacks against Portuguese strongholds and raid their ships. They were to set their flags down at Goa, claim the western state of India, and lace knots in all the loose ends of Dutch-Indian trade agreements. They were also expected to do the same in the Malaysian state of Malacca and expel the Spanish traders there by any means necessary.

In spite of the VOC's unwavering determination to conquer the Asian ports, their efforts were stalled and ultimately fruitless. The naval troops headed by Cornelis Matelief de Jong were met with violent resistance in Malacca in 1606. To rub salt in the wound, after much negotiation, Matelief failed to reach a conclusive agreement with Chinese officials on Amsterdam-China trade relations.

Matelief

The only Portuguese port that conceded without a fight was one based in the naturally rich and fertile Ambon Island. There, the VOC set up camp with a new headquarters and placed the island under Dutch administration. Unlike Matelief, van der Hagen presented a signed contract in which the island promised to sell cloves exclusively to the VOC. The agreement would become a basis for all future VOC transactions.

Meanwhile, the Dutch were in the midst of the Eighty Years War, a long battle of independence against Spain. Though Matelief's ships had yielded less than pleasing results, the Dutch knew outdated enemy vessels were no match for the VOC's newly improved ships. In the late months of 1606, the Dutch States General ordered an attack against Iberian vessels loitering in European waters, and a year later, Dutch vessels overtook a much larger fleet of Spanish warships. With the Spanish defenses badly bruised, the government of Madrid raised a white flag. For the next 2 years, Dutch and Madrid government officials assembled in underground meetings, and their efforts led to the publishing of the Twelve Years' Truce.

The Dutch government knew that the truce – though vocally opposed by Prince Maurice and the VOC – had to be reached for a number of reasons. For one, pepper prices were plummeting and failing to recover. The loss at the standoff against the Spanish in the Philippines, Maluku Islands, Flanders, and other conflicts the Dutch had engaged in had taken a toll on the weakening army population as well. Moreover, competition was getting fiercer by the minute, and rumors had been circulating about France's King Henry IV looking to start an East Indian Company of his own with the help of Flemish and Dutch traitors.

Henry IV

With the newly-established truce underway, the VOC shifted their focus back to the east, and the company's ships began to explore the other nations bordering the coasts of Southeast Asia. Early encounters with Japanese and Chinese locals were met with much hostility and little success, but the undeterred VOC resumed the expeditions. During this time, they attacked and established bases in Macau and the Philippines, and inadvertently discovered the continent of Australia.

As the VOC continued the journey around Southeast Asia, bases were strategically scattered around the region. Since most Indonesian merchants only accepted rare textiles from the Coromandel Coast, situated by the borders of the Indian subcontinent, Dutch factories were placed near the seaside of Golconda, India. A year later, in 1606, a Dutch post was constructed in Northwestern India for the easy trading of indigo and cotton.

Following the announcement of the truce in 1608, VOC authorities ordered its crew to handle all unresolved trade agreements as soon as possible. When VOC ships failed to infiltrate Portuguese crews at Macau for the second time, they moved on to Japan. After a few months of "negotiation," the VOC came to an exclusive trade agreement with a factory in Hirado.

Later that year, the VOC revisited the Maluku Islands and signed another treaty there. By the time the short-lived truce disintegrated in April 1609, the VOC had established as many Asian outposts as their competition. Though most of the Portuguese regions had been conquered, the VOC had yet to strike down the Iberian bases in Macau, Malacca, Manila, Ternate, and Goa.

The VOC needed to accelerate their growing control over Asian trade, lest they be wiped out by the vehement competition. In 1610, the VOC created the position of the Governor General. The Governor General was now to be considered the highest of all authorities in Dutch rule over the East Indies. The first to take on the mammoth responsibilities of the Governor General was veteran voyager Admiral Pieter Both, who was sworn into office on the 19th of December. To curb the somewhat tyrannical powers of the Governor General, a board known as the Raad van Indie, or "Council of the Indies," was set in place. That said, though the Governor General spearheaded all activities in the East Indies, all decisions and matters were still to be approved by the Heeren XVII.

Both

Batavia and Yonder

"Despair not, spare your enemies not, for God is with us." – Jan Pieterszoon Coen

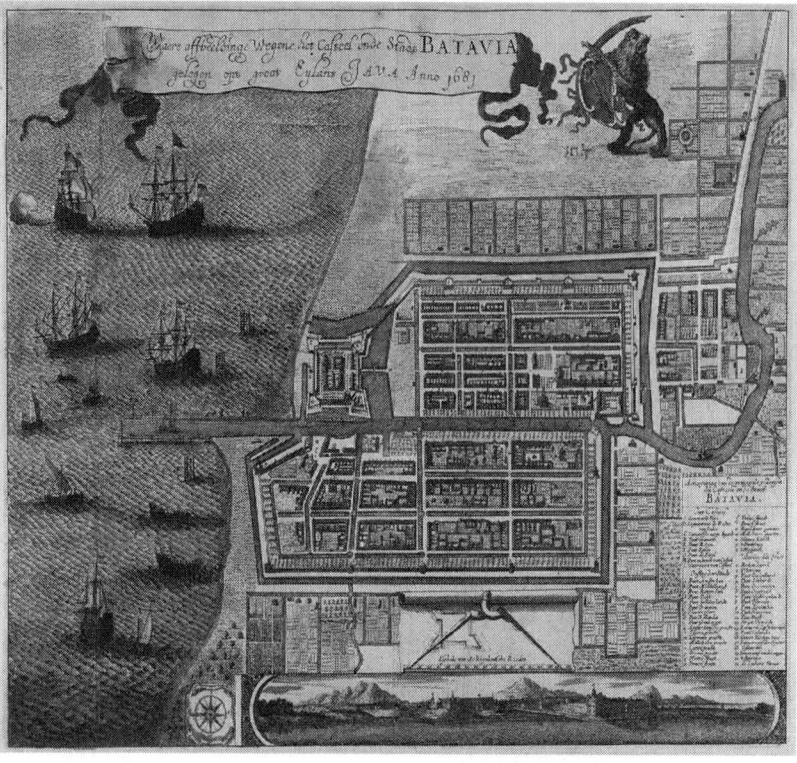

17th century maps depicting Batavia

To understand the VOC's unfaltering interest over the Indonesian islands, one particular spice must be assessed – the nutmeg. Before the VOC even existed, these toffee-brown, aromatic seeds had become a raging hit in Europe. Nutmegs, like peppers, were highly versatile, especially since the seeds were used not just to flavor drinks and desserts but also as a scent freshener.

Apart from masking the pungent stenches that wafted from poorly preserved meats, the spice was praised by European physicians for its alleged medicinal properties. During the second coming of the infamous Black Death, which struck Europe throughout the 17th century, experts pointed to the nutmeg as a cure and plague repellent. Sachets and smelling vials bottled with eau de nutmeg were prescribed to all. Young ladies were often seen sniffing these trinkets to avoid the toxicity thick in the air. Men sprinkled nutmeg into their nasal powders, otherwise known as "snuff," and inhaled the spice's fiery, invigorating goodness.

The demand for nutmeg was sensational, particularly in London, which had suffered the worst of the roving plague. English consumers were desperate to get their hands on the spice, and willing to pay up to twice their paychecks for a few grams of nutmeg. Simultaneously, merchants and traders were reaping in the profits. To put this into perspective, for a bulk 10 pound order of nutmeg, an English merchant shelled out a total of 1 English penny to their Asian suppliers. This sum, which translates to about $3.74 USD today, was then marked up to 2 pounds and 11 shillings (roughly $790 USD) to the average London consumer.

Learning of the English merchants' jaw-dropping profit margins, the VOC decided a change of priorities was in order. Nutmeg was perhaps one of the scarcest, and hence most treasured of the world's spices. As far as the 17th century world knew, there was only one place in all the world that housed the beloved nutmeg trees: the Banda Islands of Indonesia. The VOC did its homework on the islands and performed a background check on the reigning sultans. They learned of the government's neutral trade agreements with foreign traders, which allowed them to trade freely with vessels regardless of nation or continent. While this meant that Portuguese and Spanish garrisons were no longer allowed on Bandanese soil, the VOC took advantage of the island's virtually defenseless coast.

In late 1618, 31-year-old Jan Pieterszoon Coen was named Governor General of the VOC. The slender, dark-haired man with vigilant, beady eyes and a thin, well-groomed mustache, embraced the honorable position with open arms. In spite of his relatively young age, the members of the Heeren XVII were confident that they had chosen the perfect candidate. Coen would soon prove them right, with his name forever remembered as one of the shrewdest and most ruthless of all the VOC's Governor Generals.

Coen

Coen was born in the charming harbor town of Hoorn, one of the 7 Dutch towns involved in the VOC. From a young age, his father, a small-time merchant, introduced Coen to the world of business, and encouraged him to pursue an interest for it. In 1601, a year before the VOC opened its doors, 14-year-old Coen was sent to Rome to study the fine art of international trade and business. For the rest of his teenage years, Coen served as an apprentice to a Dutch merchant company based in Rome, where the brilliant teenager quickly picked up and learned the trade of double-entry bookkeeping, a concept that was still foreign back in Holland. The bright eyed and bushy tailed apprentice was soon promoted to the position of Junior Merchant.

With his new title, 20-year-old Coen was sent on his first expedition to the East Indies in 1607, where he stayed for 3 years before heading back home to Holland for another 2. In 1612, Coen graduated to Senior Merchant, and as Coen's influence within the company grew alongside his confidence, he began to share his findings with his peers and superiors. The ecstatic Coen fished out a copy of the *Discoers Touscherende den Nederlantsche Indischen Staet*, the VOC's handbook of company operations. With it, he presented a detailed and insightful analysis of the handbook, complete with highlighted discrepancies.

Coen criticized the overly complex VOC system and noted its poor generation of profits compared to those of their competitors. In his analysis, he offered 2 potential solutions. To begin with, he suggested the VOC impose a monopoly over 3 main spices – mace, cloves, and nutmegs. Next, this monopoly was to be enforced at any cost, condoning the exploitation and slavery of local workers and other means of violence to generate results. A passage from Coen's analysis reads, "Your honors should know by experience that trade in Asia must be driven and maintained under the protection and favor of Your Honor's own weapons, and that weapons must be paid for by the profits from the trade, so that we cannot carry on trade without war, nor war without trade." As Coen had hoped, he was soon on the VOC's radar, especially that of the Hereen XVII's.

Even before Coen had been entrusted to lead the expedition to the Banda Islands, relations between the Bandanese and the Dutch were rocky. The Dutch's first arrival there came in 1599, and initially, the Bandanese welcomed the Dutch merchants, who were a refreshing change of pace from the aggressive Bible-toting evangelists that came with the Portuguese ships. The friendly first meeting resulted in a signed document between both parties, which granted the Dutch full and exclusive rights to the island's nutmegs at obscenely low prices. Many have speculated that the Bandanese were somehow conned into signing an agreement that they did not understand due to the obvious language barrier. Whatever the case, when the agreement came into effect, troubles began to brew.

What happened next would be one of the earliest and most compelling pieces of evidence that exhibited the VOC's merciless business tactics. They disregarded the fact that the majority of Bandanese food sources relied almost solely on trade with neighboring nations. To avoid starvation, the Bandanese went ahead and took the risk of trading with non-Dutch countries anyway. The Bandanese were then severely punished for "violating the agreement," one the Dutch knew full well they would not be able to fulfill.

During Coen's first year in office, he decided it was time to give the Indonesian islands another whirl. On May 30, 1619, Coen, along with a daunting fleet of 19 armed ships, invaded Jayakarta (now Jakarta). The VOC's men, equipped with the best military equipment, cleared out the Jayakarta residents and Banten forces guarding the coast with seemingly minimal effort. Here, Coen ordered the VOC crew to begin construction of the new overseas headquarters. At first, the original trading post, which was built 16 years prior, was treated to simple cosmetic touch-ups and a slight expansion. But less than 2 months later, in mid-July, the blueprints for the new VOC fortress were updated yet another time, and as soon as the blueprints were approved, the second round of renovations began. Now, a much larger red-bricked castle stood in place of the original trading post, towering over the island. Bastions, or tall, sturdy walls, were paved around the coastal edge of the castle to defend the fortress from naval attacks. A collection of hired soldiers from various countries including Germany, Scotland, Belgium, and Japan patrolled the headquarters around the clock. In the basement was a dingy torture cellar, its walls brimming with ropes, iron shackles, and water-boarding equipment.

Coen proposed a name for the VOC fortress. He hoped to call the place "Nieuw-Hoorn" (New

Hoorn), a tribute to his hometown. The Hereen XVII, however, voted against it, electing to call it "Batavia," instead. The name, which rolled off the tongue like honey, stuck, and in January of 1621, a formal christening ceremony was held.

Before, during, and after Coen's reign as Governor General, 3 branches of administration would arise within Batavia. The first branch, the Hoge Regering (High Government), came into prominence 6 years after the first Banten takeover, in 1609. This branch placed at the top of the tier, composed of the Governor General and the Council of the Indies. Next was the College van Schepenen (Council of Aldermen), established under Coen's request in 1620. The small board consisted of "3 free citizens" and 2 VOC officials. The final branch was the College van Heemraden (District Council), which came to be much later in the mid-17th century.

Now that Batavia was established as a Dutch stronghold, administrative center, and main trading port of the VOC, a community soon flourished within and around the fortress. To make room for more Dutch plantations, the Javanese were banished from Batavia. Almost all of the natives were either expelled, killed, or wasted away from starvation. No Dutch families had immigrated to Batavia, so the Batavian population became a kind of melting pot. Though Coen had enforced a violent restraining order against the Javanese people, some of the Dutch began to pair off with what was left of the Javanese locals.

Coen would go on to personally request a shipment of 1,000 Chinese people from Macau to diversify the growing Batavian community. Unfortunately, only a small fraction of 1,000 would survive the trip. 2 years later, another request for 15,000 Bandanese people ended in more tragedy. Just 600 of the 15,000 would reach the Batavian shore.

Mishaps and Mutiny

"The pack of all disasters has molded together and fallen on my neck." – Francesco Pelsaert

Around this time, the Dutch government attempted to resolve the churning tensions between the VOC and the British East India Company. In 1619, King James I and the States General of Netherlands shook hands, vowing a unified collaboration of trade in the East Indies. Each side would be allotted a fixed ratio of 2:1 in the Asian trade market, which was balanced by the legal monopolies both parties held in their home countries. The Batavian Council of Defense had been established for the very reason of supervising both the Dutch and English merchants. Both parties agreed to trade benevolently alongside each other, with outposts on each side left to govern themselves.

James I

Not surprisingly, it would not take long before growing disputes of the treaty's terms threatened their peaceful relations. Dutch outposts claimed legal jurisdiction over British posts in their regions. On the other hand, the British cited the treaty terms and demanded the Dutch withdraw their prying noses from British posts. The tensions began to snowball, and the avalanche of disagreements soured the relationship between the two companies. The Dutch began to regard the English as dishonest and unscrupulous, and vice versa. Each accused the other of selfishly interpreting and thereby manipulating the treaty to its own liking.

The bubbling animosity was not helped by a memo Herman van Speult sent out in 1622. Van Speult, a prominent VOC player based in Ambon Island, had began to butt heads with the Sultan rulers of Ternate. The sultan, Van Speult suspected, had been plotting to back out of the Dutch-Ternate trade agreement, and was looking to jump the Dutch ship. For this, van Speult blamed the British, who he firmly believed was the puppeteer behind the scenes.

The VOC officials on Ambon Island heeded Van Speult's warnings and began to grow paranoid. In February of 1623, a Japanese soldier-for-hire was caught red-handed and accused of spying on a Dutch base, Victoria. The soldier was hauled into the underground torture chamber and his limbs forcibly tethered to the sides of a wooden board. As a filthy sack was pulled over the soldier's head, VOC crewmen poured barrels of water over his head, nearly suffocating him. Through an excruciating stretch of water torture, otherwise known as waterboarding, they were able to extract a confession from the soldier. The gurgling captive admitted to being part of a band of 20 mercenaries employed by the British East India Company. The soldiers were allegedly hired to sneak into Fortress Victoria and assassinate Van Speult. He went on to point a finger at Gabriel Towerson, a nearby governor for an English base, and other members of staff.

After that, the rest of the soldiers and accused English personnel were dragged in to the Dutch base for another torture session. William Clarke, one of the Englishmen, was one of those who suffered the worst of the tortures. In addition to flogging, VOC officials "cruelly cut his flesh, then washed him with salt and vinegar" before laying him upon a bed of scalding-hot irons.

Archived records show that 4 Englishmen and 2 Japanese soldiers evaded further punishment and were pardoned for reasons unknown. The rest of the condemned, a group that consisted of 10 Englishmen, 9 Japanese mercenaries, and 1 Portuguese soldier, were sentenced to death. On the 9th of March, the group was beheaded. In an effort to prevent future conspiracies, Towerson's severed head was pierced upon a pole and flaunted around in a morbid parade around Ambon Island.

Another significant chapter in VOC history came in the form of a terrible mutiny in 1629. On the 4th of June, the VOC ship *Batavia* crashed on the Abrolhos Islands, just 37 miles from Geraldton, Australia. The 316 dazed passengers on board poured out of the dead vessel, thanking the Heavens as their feet touched solid ground. Little did they know of the horrors that were soon to come.

Picture of a replica of the *Batavia*

On October 28, 1628, the VOC's *Batavia* set sail from Texel in the Northern Netherlands. The vessel was a humdinger, a polished wooden ship kitted out with dozens of bronze guns and 24 cast-iron cannons. Along with 7 other ships, the VOC vessels took on the salty, frigid waters, destined for Batavia.

A few characters must be introduced to understand what led up to the horrific event. There was Francesco Pelsaert, a senior merchant who was in charge of the Batavia. Next, there was Adriaen Jacobsz, the ship's skipper, or second-in-command. Jacobsz cried conspiracy, faulting the system for placing a merchant over an experienced ship captain – which he was – in command. Naturally, the pair never got along. Of the 300-plus passengers aboard, a few more figures would play a significant role in the upcoming incident. There was a young woman named Lucretia van der Mijlen, who was reuniting with her husband in Batavia. Zwaantje Hendrix, Lucretia's maid, had also scored a seat on the ship. Finally, there was the middle-ranking merchant, Jeronimus Cornelisz.

Jacobsz, whose charm failed to beguile the happily married Miljen, turned to Hendrix for romantic comfort. This pair would hit it off. Miljen, put off by Jacobsz's boldness, approached

Pelsaert. Bonded by a mutual dislike for Jacobsz, they soon became fast friends.

Having to spend time with a sworn enemy is never smooth sailing, and this was certainly the case for the bickering Jacobsz and Pelsaert. As months passed by, Jacobsz's resentment for Pelsaert began to grow. He began to daydream about what it would be like to overthrow Pelsaert and claim the ship as his own, after which he could pursue a life of piracy, thrilling adventures, and unimaginable riches across the seas. He confided in Cornelisz, who shared his sentiments.

The *Batavia* paused for a pit stop at the Cape of Good Hope in mid-April of 1629. Here, the VOC crew took some time off to let down their hair and unwind. Jacobsz took this to the extreme. Jacobsz, accompanied by Cornelisz and his fling, Hendrix, went on week-long drinking binges. The trio's hard partying resulted in pricey damages to wrecked pubs and other damaged property. As Pelsaert's ears rang with the complaints from crewmen and the Cape's residents, he summoned Jacobsz and rebuked him furiously.

When the *Batavia* resumed its journey, an even more embittered Jacobsz began to hold secret meetings with his partner-in-crime, Cornelisz. The pair became determined to turn their fantasies to reality. They concocted a plan – assemble a group of rebels, do away with those who opposed them, and feed Pelsaert to the ravenous sharks circling under them. They would then take control of the ship and all its booty, and disappear in the Indies.

By the time June came along, the plan was set in motion. Under the conspirators' orders, a group of rebel crewmen cornered Miljen and sexually assaulted her. The traumatized and hysterical Miljen managed to escape and ran straight to Pelsaert. As expected, Miljen recognized at least one of her attackers, and the livid Pelsaert sought out to right the injustice at once, a signal for the conspirators to reach their next milestone.

In a twist of events, the *Batavia* suddenly crashed into Abrolhos Island. Multiple attempts failed to salvage the ship, and the hopeless vessel started to sink. The conspirators' plan was thwarted – for now. The majority of the passengers would survive the crash, and sought refuge in nearby islands. Unluckily for them, the barren islands were unforgiving, with little to no clean, consumable water. In the face of disaster, Pelsaert and Jacobsz set their differences aside and launched 2 boats with 48 crewmen to the mainland on the hunt for drinkable water. They searched far and wide, but could not locate a legitimate water supply.

Discouraged, the 48 crewmen set off for Batavia, hoping to strengthen the aid. Again, most would survive the trip, and would arrive at the VOC headquarters in July. Here, Jacobsz, along with a few of the accused attackers of Miljen, were arrested, tried, and charged with negligence and unruly behavior. Pelsaert was then tasked to fetch the rest of the survivors in Abrolhos on another VOC vessel, the Sardam.

Back at Abrolhos, many of the survivors had perished from thirst and starvation. Cornelisz, now the highest-ranking official by default among the shipwrecked in Abrolhos, decided it was time to take action – with or without Jacobsz. But first, he sent Wiebbe Hayes and his loyal troop of 20 soldiers onto another island in search of food and supplies.

With Hayes, who he suspected would give him trouble, out of his hair, Cornelisz acted fast. He activated his fellow conspirators, and together, the mutineers confiscated all weapons and whatever little food and supplies were left. The survivors had no choice but to submit, as those who so much as questioned Cornelisz and his men were viciously slaughtered. For weeks, people were drowned, battered, and gutted – including women and children. The conspirators hoped to set an example for potential insubordinates.

Hayes grew suspicious when his smoke signals went unanswered, and it was only then that the mutiny began to unravel. The moment Hayes and his men learned about the ongoing massacre and rogue tyrants, they, along with the arriving Sardam rescue vessel, ended the mutiny. At this point, 125 people had been tortured, raped, and senselessly murdered. All the conspirators were rounded up, shackled, and shipped back to Batavia. The VOC vowed to make the men pay for their crimes, a move that hinted at the company's overall solidarity. Cornelisz had his hands lopped off before he was executed. The rest of the conspirators suffered the latter fate.

A contemporary depiction of the executions

Hayes was later commemorated as a hero, receiving awards and a promotion to Sergeant. Pelsaert was left to take the blame for the mutiny, and all of his belongings and finances would be locked down by the VOC. A year later, he died a penniless laughingstock.

Siege

"An empire founded by war has to maintain itself by war." – Charles de Montesquieu

At this point, the VOC, with only the company's constant growth in mind, continued to learn from past mistakes, and Governor General Coen in particular can be credited with unearthing another crucial problem in the company's shortcomings. Coen believed he had identified the reason behind the strained business relations between Asia and Europe. Asian consumers only had an appetite for European silver and gold, but these precious metals, which were aplenty in Spain and Portugal, were rare on Dutch and British soil. Soon, the Asian consumers began to reject the VOC currency, expecting to be paid in gold and silver for the spices they provided. Both the Dutch and British companies knew the only feasible solution to this problem would be to maintain a trade surplus. This meant that the price of Asian spices had to be sold at a marked up price in local Dutch and British markets. It was Coen who suggested that the profits made from their new monopoly on the Asian trade be reinvested into the company. This, he believed, would keep the European market afloat. The VOC did just that, a practice that would continue on to 1630.

Now older and wiser, the VOC decided it was time to take on the rest of the Asian market. Towards the mid-17th century, the VOC created a thriving network of trading posts, planting a flag in hot spots far and wide across the Asian map. The Batavia headquarters received shipments from their home base of supplies to furnish the needs of local crewmen. Silver, copper, and jewelry from Japan were used to barter for Indian and Chinese spices, silk, porcelain, cotton, and other rare textiles. The arsenal of the VOC's Asian products would be used to purchase shiploads of cotton, which would then be transported back to the Netherlands. At the same time, the VOC crew made sure to form steady and tactical relationships with Asian locals. They exchanged modern European ideas and technology with Asian merchants, and engaged in religious philanthropy. The trust built up within these relationships would soon play in their favor.

VOC officials came to a mutually-appealing agreement with the Tokugawa Shogunate, the last feudal military government – of Dejima Island in Nagasaki, Japan. In 1638, the head of the Tokugawa enforced the "Sakoku," which translates to the "Closed Door Policy." The decree shunned all Portuguese residents from the man-made island, which had been built for the Portuguese forces in the first place. 3 years later, the VOC evacuated their previous post in Hirado and permanently moved in to Dejima, the new VOC headquarters in Japan. For 200 years, Dejima would remain the only place where Europeans were allowed to conduct Japanese trade.

Things did not go over as smoothly with the Chinese. In 1623, a VOC official traveled to China in the hopes of convincing the Ming Dynasty to grant the Dutch exclusive use of the Penghu Islands. When the Chinese refused to comply with VOC terms, a mini-war between the Chinese and the Dutch ensued, one that lasted until 1662. In this instance, the VOC agreed that brute force was the only answer. The lush greenery and peaceful quiet of the Penghu Islands were disrupted in the early morning of late 1623 as VOC officials barged into the islands, seizing the territory and erecting a makeshift fort. The Chinese military instantly appeared on the scene and retaliated, eventually emerging victorious a year later. In 1633, the VOC tried their luck a second time, but the company was once again defeated in the Battle of Liaoluo Bay.

The VOC's losing streak continued into the 1640s, thanks this time to the Cambodians. In 1643, at the height of the Trinh-Nguyen War, wherein the local Trinh clan resisted the reigning Mac Dynasty, Cambodian soldiers blew up a VOC vessel, killing everyone on board.

That same year, the VOC would suffer another devastating loss. Back in 1637, the VOC had established a base in Cambodia; the VOC had effectively dominated the Japanese market, and aspired to do the same in Cambodia. The Dutch base in Cambodia was built in the Japanese neck of the country, which further convinced the Dutch that this would be a cakewalk. With that in mind, the VOC was unaware that Japanese mercenaries made up most of their town. Their relationship with the Portuguese was one that long predated that of Dutch-Cambodian relations. Members of the census also included Japanese Catholics and Black-Portuguese, with relatives and ancestors from Goa, Ceylon, and Africa.

Up until 1642, all 3 parties to the equation lived in harmony. The Dutch and Cambodian trade was profitable on both sides, as was the prospering trade and relations between Japan and Cambodia. All that came crashing down when Cambodian Prince Ramathipothei, an unstable 22-year-old tyrant, rose to the throne. In his quest to take the crown, he found allies in Malaysian, Japanese, and Portuguese mercenaries, who helped him slash his way to the throne. The new king was no fan of the Cambodia-based director, Pieter van Regemortes, and by extension, the VOC. In early 1642, a VOC vessel captured a pair of Portuguese cargo ships at the mouth of the Mekong River and looted them clean. The king, who favored the Portuguese merchants, ordered Van Regemortes to reimburse the Portuguese. Van Regemortes countered with an under-the-table bribe. The king accepted the bribe and dusted his hands clean of the incident. That said, the wary VOC director set off for Batavia, where he unloaded his concerns about the king to Governor General van Dieman. Van Dieman promoted Van Regemortes to ambassador and urged him to return to Cambodia.

Juiced up with the power of his new ambassadorial status, Van Regemortes arrived in Udong in November of 1643. He made a beeline for the Cambodian castle and personally handed the king a letter from the Governor General. In the scornful letter, Van Dieman demanded the bribe to be paid back in full. If the king failed to meet the VOC's demands, the company threatened to wage war on Cambodia and remove all goods from their Dutch base, effective immediately. After a quick scan of the letter, the brooding king coolly organized a follow-up meeting with the VOC, setting the date on the 27th of November.

When the day came, the king and his men massacred the unsuspecting Van Regemortes and his staff. Later that day, the king broke into the Dutch base, butchered each and every one of the factory staff, and made off with all of the inventory. Meanwhile, Cambodian warships captured 2 more VOC vessels and imprisoned all crew members. At least 50 Dutch civilians and soldiers lost their lives in the bloodbath, and another 60 or so were thrown behind bars.

Burned by the losing streak and fueled by a burgeoning hatred for the Portuguese, who the VOC deemed to be the root of their problems, things began to pick up. Back in 1640, the trading posts the VOC planted along the coasts of Ceylon and Galle tipped the scale against the Portuguese, marking the point their monopoly on cinnamon died. 12 years later, a second trading post was built in the Cape of Good Hope, which would provide supplies for the VOC in and around South Africa. Another triumph came in 1652, when the VOC partnered up with Sri Lankan King of Kandy and dominated the Colombo market.

In 1659, the VOC drove the Portuguese out of their stations in the Malabar Coast and claimed it as their own. This ensured that the Portuguese were never to fulfill their dream of conquering Sri Lanka, or any part of Western India for that matter. By 1663, the Portuguese were left with a single trading post in all of the west coast of India. More VOC stations founded at this point were located in Bengal, Siam, Persia, Malabar, and Formosa.

A depiction of the VOC station at Bengal

Yet another siege would soon arise, this time in the vibrant and mountainous terrain of Formosa. The VOC first arrived in Formosa after losing at Penghu in 1624. Now known as Taiwan, the island was described as "a good milking cow for the [VOC]." Records show that the company made a gross profit of 330,000 guilders ($33 million USD) in 1653 from the Formosan market alone. By 1632, 2 more VOC outposts had popped up in the peninsula of Taoyuan (Fort Zeelandia) and another at a nearby bay (Fort Provintia).

In 1659, Koxinga, a Ming supporter and resistor to the Qing Dynasty, started a quest to find a new headquarters overseas. When word got around to a Chinese VOC crewman named Ho-Bin, the man journeyed to Xiamen with a scroll of Formosa's map tucked under his arm. On April 2, 1661, Koxinga, along with a trained crew of 25,000, stormed into Taoyuan. The bloody takeover wreaked havoc among the Dutch, local, and aboriginal communities of Formosa. By the next year, almost all of the Dutch presence had been forced out of Formosa.

A year later, the VOC made another breakthrough. Caught in the middle of a raging conflict between the Aceh Sultanate and Indonesian lords, the VOC knew it would be wise to take a side. They ceased trade with the sultanate, veering their business towards the locals. The new relationship was solidified with the 1663 Treaty of Painan. There, the VOC built an outpost and was able to monopolize the trade of gold, tin, and pepper.

By 1669, the VOC was the largest and richest private company to have ever existed. The company's roster boasted a staff of 50,000 employees and 10,000 mercenaries around the globe, with 150 merchant vessels and 40 fully-equipped warships. As the VOC entered the 18th century, however, things would take a dark turn.

Fall from Grace

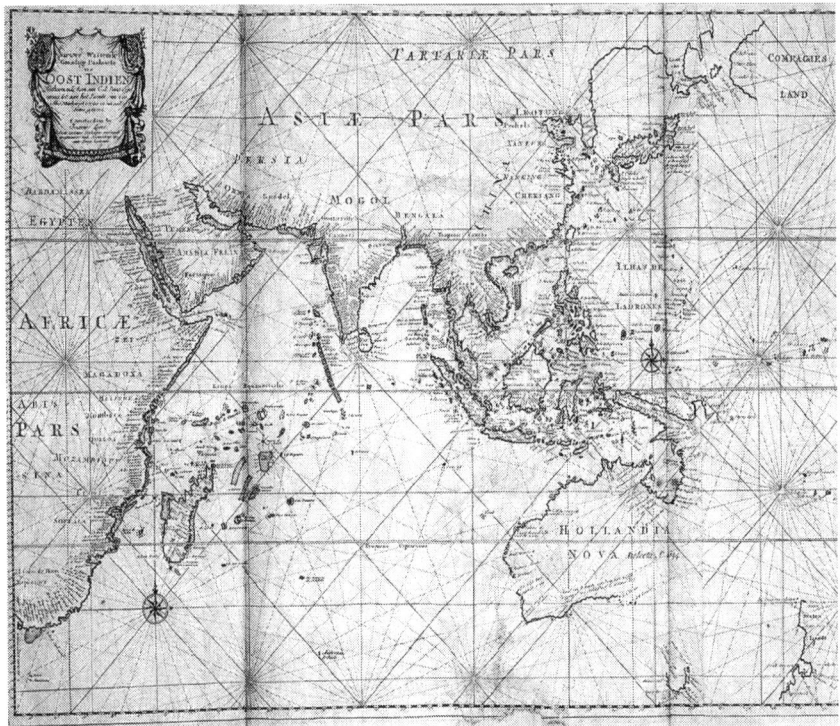

A map of the VOC's area of operations around 1700

"Failure comes only when we forget our ideals and objectives and principles." – Jawaharlal Nehru, Prime Minister of India

By the 1670s, the steady progress of the VOC was quickly losing steam. For one, the company was still wincing from the fresh wounds caused by the Siege of Zeelandia. China's conversion from the Qing Dynasty to the Ming only intensified the inflammation, which brought about the end of Sino-Dutch silk trade in 1666. To make matters worse, business with their most profitable Asian channel, Japan, was beginning to decline.

In a futile attempt at damage control, the VOC hastened to make adjustments. To make up for the loss of the Chinese silk trade, the VOC sought out an alternative in Bengali merchants, but not only were the profits from the Bengali market nowhere close to those made from the Chinese, their main supply of Japanese silver, gold, and precious metals was slipping from their grasp. Despite more useless attempts at reeling in the rope, the Dejima Shogunate imposed a series of decrees that limited the trade between Japan and the Netherlands. By 1685, the VOC's presence in Japan was no more.

As the VOC entered the 18th century, it appeared that a change of good tide was about to come. After much debate, the Heeren XVII chose to increase fortification in all the VOC outposts along the Malabar Coast. In 1710, the VOC officials captured the Zamorin of Calicut, a royal title used by the monarchs of the Kozhikode Kingdom. The company proceeded to physically coerce the Hindu royal to kneel before his Dutch captors.

With Dutch hands firmly wrapped around the royal's fist, the Zamorin signed a treaty that declared trade exclusivity between the VOC and the kingdom, and the VOC relished in the profits reaped from the treaty's terms for 5 years before the British East India Company intervened. With the rival company's support, the treaty was shredded to pieces. The VOC would hold down their fort for a few more years before deciding that the Malabar Coast was no longer worth the effort. In 1721, the VOC surrendered their territory on the coast to the British.

Perhaps the most significant and withering of the blows that struck the VOC came 2 decades later. August 10, 1741 marked the first time an Asian power had fought back against the Dutch, or any European conquerors, since the start of the Age of Exploration. The fight was henceforth known as the Battle of Colachel, with the Kingdom of Travancore going head to head with the VOC. With the home court advantage, this would be the first and last time an Indian kingdom emerged victorious over a European army. Likewise, this was the first and only time where an Asian naval force defeated a European fleet.

1741 would be the year the VOC officially relinquished its hold over the Indian market. It was no longer possible to rely on the company's "low volume-high profit" business model. On top of that, the turn of the century had brought a change of European taste in commodities as well; the European consumers' attraction to the VOC's selection of Asian coffee, tea, textiles, and porcelain was starting to wane, and with that the VOC approached its inevitable demise.

In fact, the VOC's aforementioned attempts at expansion in the early 18th century turned out to be a recipe for disaster. The VOC started to feel the holes that had been burned through their pockets. To compensate for the growing volume of stock and overhead the company was now handling, they built stronger and larger ships. Regrettably, the insufficient manpower and fall in labor productivity not only stumped the growth of the company, it threatened its very existence. The VOC's conundrum was what historians labeled "profitless growth." To add on to the VOC's increasing instability in Asia, company morale was at its lowest point. Hours were long, and staff groused about their low wages.

What was more, of all the East India Companies, the VOC seemed to have been cursed with the highest employee death tolls. As the VOC's profits ebbed every year, the morbid statistics climbed, seeing more staff killed by disease or warfare than its rival companies. Their stagnant growth in the company had also become a major turn-off, as the upper management banned staff from trading outside of the office. Perhaps unsurprisingly, corruption began to run rampant within the company.

Most important of all was the amount of debt the VOC had been racking up over the years. By 1780, the company was worth 74 million guilders (approximately $7.4 billion USD today), with 28 million in ships and inventory, and the trading fund and inventory bound for Europe making up the other 46 million. Their total debt, however, was at a teeth-chattering 62 million total. At this stage, steps could have been taken to put the debt to sleep if not for the Fourth-Anglo Dutch War of 1784. During the conflict, British forces invaded VOC settlements in both Europe and Asia, which eliminated more than half of the VOC fleet. The fantastic damage added another 43 million guilders to the wobbling company's already crushing debt, and the company's net assets were now totally worthless.

A riot in Batavia and the emerging power of Brazil undercutting the Dutch merchants sealed the fate of the VOC's collapse. Following the Batavian riot in 1740, which saw the ruin and carnage of 10,000 Chinese locals, the Heeren XVII conducted an in-depth investigation into the VOC and Dutch government for the very first time. The investigation stoked the flames of the VOC's degeneration.

No matter which way they swung, the VOC could not glue the pieces back together. On March 1, 1796, ownership of the company was passed on to the Batavian Republic. On December 31, 1799, the VOC's charter officially expired.

The Aftermath

"We travel, some of us forever, to seek other states, other lives, other souls." – Anaïs Nin

Apart from the government-sanctioned torture and thousands of deaths that ensued during the VOC's reign, lurking behind the veil of the Dutch monopoly was a barrage of hidden controversies.

As an appetizer, the Dutch East India Company was directly involved in the world's first ever market crash. This incident is now infamously remembered as "Tulip Mania." During this time, the Netherlands was enjoying the enrichment in culture and wealth that came with the 17th century Dutch Golden Age, and the city of Amsterdam was the nation's commercial hub, owing its gratitude to the then-thriving VOC. In addition to the fragrant spices, blue glass, and fine china from Asia, the tulip flower became another highly sought after luxury item. Not wanting to miss out on the new hot commodity, the VOC began to dabble in tulip trading on the side. All over Europe, consumers were hopelessly smitten with the colorful flowers that came in a delightful range of brilliant, vivid colors, and it soon became a symbol associated with the European upper class.

Between 1634 and 1637, tulip bulbs experienced a head-scratching surge in prices. A single bulb, which used to cost a single guilder, was now priced at 60. This amounted to about 10 times the annual income of an average craftsman, and thus, dishonest merchants got into the habit of dealing solely in the tulip business. Many sold off the rest of their stock to sell tulips at ridiculously marked up prices, making more than they could ever hope for with their former business models. The market finally imploded in winter of 1637, at which point the bulbs were now worth only a hundredth of its original price.

Most concerning of the criticisms was the VOC's promotion of slavery. Records estimate that anywhere between 660,000-1,135,000 slaves were used by the company in its nearly 2 century long reign. Ironically, many of the Dutch who longed for the riches and resources that could be found on Asian soil harbored prejudices against Asian communities, and many of the wealthiest Dutch merchants who settled in Asia hosted a staff of at least 200 slaves. The Dutch help were instructed to work in the front of the estate, whereas the Asians were strictly confined to the back of the house. As a matter of fact, some historians alleged that the only reason for the influx of multicultural communities within the VOC was simply because there were no European women.

Another researcher offers a stark statistic – over half the Batavian population consisted of VOC slaves. Dutch slaves were freed upon the deaths of their masters, and they were only legitimized if this was specified in their master's will. The only things that did not discriminate were the constant diseases that plagued the VOC communities, which wiped out equal numbers of slaves and Dutch merchants alike.

The VOC would also leave a lasting imprint in modern day Indonesia. One example lies in the "race pyramid" that still exists in Indonesian society today. Those with Dutch blood are placed on the top, followed by Javanese nobility and the middle-ranking Chinese. Indigenous Malaysians place last on the lowest level of the pyramid. Both the Catholic Portuguese and the Protestant Dutch would have an impact on the nation's religion as well. Catholicism and Protestantism are part of the 6 official religions in Indonesia today, and many of the historical Dutch settlements are still preserved throughout the country.

Like many of the largest and most influential corporations, the VOC has gained its share of praise and condemnation. At the apex of the company's impressive lifespan, the VOC is estimated to have been worth at least $7.4 trillion in 2012 US dollars (adjusted for inflation). Only one fact remains indisputable – whether one praises or criticizes the behemoth, or both, the Dutch East India Company remains the most valuable company in all of human history over 200 years after its demise.

The British East India Company

Trade Before the East India Company

The Indian Ocean has been the site of constant long-distance trade endeavors for most of recorded history. Since the days of the Roman Empire, established trade networks have connected the Indian subcontinent, Southeast Asian kingdoms in present-day Indonesia and Malaysia, and China. The period between the fall of the Western Roman Empire and the conquest of the New World in the sixteenth century is often considered a low point for European civilizations, although the concept of the "Dark Ages" has fallen out of favor. Even those who reject the idea that Europe fell into a dismal dark age still acknowledge, however, that no European state during the Middle Ages was a world power on the same scale as those found in Asia, North Africa, and the Middle East during the same period. The time coinciding with the European Middle Ages was in fact a high point for several civilizations; the highly prosperous Tang Dynasty ruled China, the Abbasids united much of the Middle East, and powerful Muslim dynasties achieved control over North Africa. During a period in which Europeans struggled to preserve older knowledge from the days of Ancient Greece and the Roman Empire, scholars in Asia and the Middle East made major new discoveries in areas like medicine, optics, and mathematics. Many of these discoveries, such as those involving astronomy, facilitated long-distance travel and trade. In short, the period preceding the rise of the modern European empires was a moment in which Asian and Middle Eastern kingdoms established stable and prosperous trade networks connecting different regions (Abu Lughod, "The World System," 80-81; Bentley, *Old World,* 33).

An understanding of Asian trade networks is not a mere prelude to the arrival of the East India Company but was also crucial for how the East India Company operated. The merchants employed by the East India Company did not create new trade networks in their efforts to secure East Asian goods from their factories in India and Southeast Asia; instead, they tapped into existing trade networks already employed by Asian merchant communities. The long existence of trade between rival kingdoms and empires also provides important context for understanding why Asian monarchs were not initially alarmed by the presence of Europeans in the region and why they did not unify their large armies to drive out the relatively small number of European interlopers, as trade networks had long survived changing power dynamics and the rise of new dynasties. The arrival of the East India Company and its early conquests in India, rather than signaling a change in global power relations, at first seemed to be consistent with previous waves of foreign dynasties that had conquered new territories and joined in the old trade networks (Wolpert, *A New History*, 126-134).

Europeans had been seeking Asian spices, silks, and other goods since at least the Middle Ages. Prior to the early modern period, most of these products had to be transported along the Silk Road connecting China to South Asia and Europe. While trade between these regions existed, it was at a smaller scale compared to the trade within and between the major Asian empires. This was largely due to the relatively poor nature of European goods; European civilizations simply did not produce anything of comparable value to Asian goods. In addition, transporting goods across land meant that each commodity changed hands several times between East Asia and its eventual European consumer; as a result, only the wealthiest members of European society could afford to purchase items like silk and pepper (Blaut, *Colonizer's Model*).

This imbalance in commodities and resources changed with the European colonization of North and South America. In South America, the Spanish found enormous quantities of silver in the Bolivian mines of Potosi. The silver bullion and other mineral wealth harvested from the conquest of the New World finally gave European nations a trading commodity that appealed to merchants and rulers in Asia. The introduction of Bolivian silver into the global economy followed quickly on the heels of expeditions such as Vasco da Gama's rounding of the Cape of Good Hope, which allowed for travel to Asia by sea instead of by land. These two factors together provided the catalyst for renewed European interest in Asian trade (See Stein, *Silver, Trade, and War*, 52). Despite increased mobility and access to resources, long-distance trade between Europe and Asia remained extremely dangerous and expensive in the 17th and 18th centuries. As it was rarely feasible for an individual merchant or small merchant company to undertake the journey, a new form of organization emerged, the joint stock company.

Vasco da Gama

The Structure of the East India Company

Although it was technically a private company rather than an organ of the British state, in some ways the East India Company operated like its own country, including engaging in such practices as diplomacy and having its own armed forces. In other ways, however, it was very much a business enterprise, the central concern of which was profit.

These two functions and their goals were sometimes directly opposed to each other; maximizing profits could lead to starvation and rebellion, while effective governance sometimes meant taking less profitable measures. This tension was constantly at work not only in India but in the interactions between the British Crown, the Court of Directors who dictated major decisions in India, and the people on the ground there. The famous politician Edmund Burke sharply criticized the East India Company while describing some of the ways it operated in a speech given in 1783: "The invariable course of the Company's policy is this: either they set up some prince too odious to maintain himself without the necessity of their assistance, or they soon render him odious by making him the instrument of their government. In that case troops are bountifully sent to him to maintain his authority. That he should have no want of assistance, a civil gentleman, called a Resident, is kept at his court, who, under pretence of providing duly for the pay of these troops, gets assignments on the revenue into his hands. Under his provident management, debts soon accumulate; new assignments are made for these debts; until, step by step, the whole revenue, and with it the whole power of the country, is delivered into his hands. The military do not behold without a virtuous emulation the moderate gains of the civil department. They feel that in a country driven to habitual rebellion by the civil government the military is necessary; and they will not permit their services to go unrewarded. Tracts of country are delivered over to their discretion. Then it is found proper to convert their commanding officers into farmers of revenue. Thus, between the well-paid civil and well-rewarded military establishment, the situation of the natives may be easily conjectured. The authority of the regular and lawful government is everywhere and in every point extinguished. Disorders and violences arise; they are repressed by other disorders and other violences. Wherever the collectors of the revenue and the farming colonels and majors move, ruin is about them, rebellion before and behind them. The people in crowds fly out of the country; and the frontier is guarded by lines of troops, not to exclude an enemy, but to prevent the escape of the inhabitants."

Burke

Since the early 18th century, the East India Company was led by a Court of Directors, usually numbering 24. This court was based in London and their base of operations was the East India House, a four-story building housed in the center of one of London's commercial districts. The Court of Directors and their staff were divided into different committees according to subject and task and they wielded immense power, with decisions affecting millions of people resting in the hands of two dozen men (Philips, 9).

A depiction of the East India House in London circa 1800

As one might imagine, passing every decision through the entire Court of Directors proved unwieldy. In addition, some issues were diplomatically or militarily sensitive and might have provoked controversy if discussed in the more public forum of the full Court. This led to the creation of a Secret Committee consisting of no more than three Directors at any given time and this committee handled time-sensitive or secretive tasks, often pertaining to diplomacy and warfare. The Secret Committee also had the closest ties with the British Crown out of all of the committees (Philips, 8).

The nature of this position changed over time, but it always consisted of a single official elected by the East India Company Court of Directors to oversee all operations within India. As of 1773, with the passage of the Regulating Act, the Governor General formally held the power to manage foreign affairs as they pertained to British interests in India. Later changes in legislation accorded the Governor General increasing authority over Indian subjects (Wolpert, New History, 307-322).

The Court of Directors, merchants, and employees of the East India Company were informally divided into two separate groups or "interests": The Indian Interest and the City and Shipping Interest. The Indian Interest included men whose involvement in the East India Company had taken them to India at some point in their lives. Most of them had lived there for a time, participated in military campaigns, and interacted with Indian subjects or trading partners. The

City and Shipping Interest, in contrast, consisted of people based in London who were involved with the shipping and mercantile side of operations rather than activities that required international travel. This second interest included warehouse owners, creditors, and others who worked in the East India Company but never saw India. Despite being involved in the same enterprise, the two interests would often clash over policy issues and the general direction of the company (Philips, 23-24).

With the exception of the elected Court of Directors, the vast majority of British people who became involved in the East India Company did so on a temporary basis. Very few people went to India with the intention of staying permanently. Instead, most merchants or sailors employed by the company went for a year or two, intending to earn a sizeable sum before they returned to Britain. In fact, few who traveled to India in the early years of the East India Company lasted more than two years, as many succumbed to malaria and other unfamiliar diseases. Those few who lasted five years were considered officially acclimated to the new environment (Farrington, Trading Places, 76). Officers were fairly well treated, but enlisted sailors received poor wages and negligible benefits. Even with the disease and poor pay, however, the experience of serving as a sailor or soldier in the East India Company was often far better than the experience of those serving in the British army or the Royal Navy.

East India Company employees in India had a range of tasks. A President oversaw each of the major regions in India, while each factory within that region had three to six employees managing its operations (Farrington, 72). Positions in India included writers (clerks), managers, and even European servants (Farrington, 76-77). Aside from those British employees who traveled to India, the East India Company also employed thousands of dockworkers in London and other British port cities. These dockworkers and sailors worked 12 hours or more per day unloading cargo from ships (Makepeace, East India Workers).

As the East India Company became more militaristic, they needed more soldiers for campaigns, and by the time the East India Company forces were absorbed into the British military in the 1870s, they had a standing army of 24,000 men. Soldiers in the employ of the East India Company were typically poor, working-class, unmarried young men. While the East India Company's army was distinct from that of the British army, the experiences of soldiers were similar in each (Levine, Prostitution, Race, and Politics, 269).

It may seem odd that the majority of people working for a foreign imperialist venture would be from India, but that was the case from the early days of the East India Company's presence in Asia. Local merchants acquired and transported goods for East India Company partners. Weavers, cloth dyers, and other workers in the textile trade formed the backbone of the factory economy (Farrington, 69-71). Later, millions would grow crops at the direction of East India Company officials (See Dutt, Economic History). Indians also made up the majority of the soldiers in the employ of the East India Company at various points. These soldiers, known as sepoys, served in campaigns against rival kingdoms and provinces. It is important to keep in mind that India prior to the 20th century was not a single country, but rather a loose collection of states and kingdoms under the umbrella of the Mughal and later the British Empire. Sepoys serving in the East India Company's forces would therefore not have conceptualized themselves as Indians fighting other Indians, but rather as soldiers of one region fighting those of a region with an entirely different language, culture, and religion (Hagerman, "Sepoy," 1005-1007).

Early History of the East India Company

A procession in Jahangir overseen by ambassador Sir Thomas Roe

The British East India Company was founded in 1600 by several London merchants through a Royal Charter from Queen Elizabeth I. The Dutch East India Company (VOC), which formed almost simultaneously, quickly had considerable successes bringing goods from Asia to Europe, while the Spanish had by far the greatest foothold in the New World and the Portuguese had been at the forefront of African and Asian exploration. Essentially, the East India Company emerged at a moment when the British appeared to be at a disadvantage compared to their European rivals.

It is important to note that despite its later significance in the formation of the British Empire, the East India Company did not initially form with colonialist motives. At its start, it focused strictly on trade by means of establishing outposts in overseas ports, forming trading partnerships with local merchants, and cornering the market on profitable goods in particular regions (Marshall, "British in Asia," 490-91). The East India Company formed during a period when similar ventures were being formed for other parts of the world; trading companies sought profits in British North America, the Pacific, and South America. While other ventures initially had more success, the East India Company eventually became the most profitable and influential.

For the first hundred years of its existence, the East India Company could hardly be considered a resounding success. It quickly landed in India and signed its first treaty with the Mughal Dynasty in 1615, securing the right to trade from a factory in Surat (Timeline). From there, they traded in textiles, indigo, cotton, and saltpeter, the last of which would eventually become one of the most important commodities to come out of India due to its use in gunpowder. However, this was at the time considered a minor achievement. At this point, the East India Company's Court of Directors had its sights on Southeast Asia rather than India, seeking to gain a foothold in places like Sumatra in order to compete against the Dutch spice trade there. These efforts were small in scale and not very profitable. A few outposts, known as factories, were established in Sumatra and other islands in the Indonesian archipelago, but these were closed down by the Dutch. Japan and China both stood out as highly desirable trading partners, but Europeans had little success there in the 17th century; Japan's Tokugawa Shogunate closed the country to all foreign traders except a handful of Dutch merchants, while China allowed foreign trade under highly controlled circumstances. In short, the major Asian empires still controlled most of the trading activities in the region. Even among European powers, the East India Company lagged behind the VOC and the Spanish Crown, which controlled the Philippines (Marshall, 490-91).

The East India Company's fortunes began to change in the early 18th century. Around 1700, East India Company merchants redirected their attention to India and established factories in several major cities, most notably Calcutta. These factories produced immense quantities of textiles and spices. In the 1720s, the profits of the East India Company finally exceeded those of the VOC as the British began to pull ahead of their European competitors in Asia. From this point on, the economy of Britain, its North American colonies, and Western Europe as a whole became heavily intertwined with Indian trade (Marshall, 490-91).

A picture of the East India Company factory at Cossimbazar

Unlike the period from the late 18th century on, the first 150 years of the East India Company's history involved few examples of regulation by the Crown or by Parliament. The company's charter had to be periodically renewed by the Crown, but the terms of the renewal in these early years were essentially limited to demands that the company remain profitable. As long as it achieved that goal, the British public and the Crown gave little thought to the details of how the East India Company operated in its factories halfway around the world.

The East India Company's approach to India changed dramatically in the 1740s. Where East India Company merchants had once been content with small outposts and factories in Mughal-controlled territories, where they had once thought more of profit than of territory, they began to act more as agents of imperial expansion.

The reasons behind this shift are complex, but one major factor was the outbreak of the Seven Years' War. The Seven Years' War, considered by some historians to be the first truly global conflict, featured warfare between Austria and Prussia in Europe and their allies, and the French and the British in the colonial theaters. The war reached the Indian Ocean in 1744 when naval battles erupted between the French and the British. Two years later, war broke out between two

Indian rulers: the Nawab (a term roughly equivalent to governor or provincial ruler) of Arcot, a British ally, and the Nizam of Hyderabad, a French ally. Operating largely as a proxy war between the two European powers, the conflict had a severe and negative impact on the local population.

At the war's end, the Nawab of Arcot stood victorious but saw his status reduced to that of a client state of the East India Company (Marshall, 492). Thus, the East India Company began to assert itself as a major figure in Indian politics and conflicts between different regional authorities. These changes coincided with similar changes in approach in the Dutch and French empires, with the new imperial turn in India coinciding with colonial efforts in Indonesia and the Pacific. Since many of the East India Company's choices abroad were driven by competition with other European states, it comes as no surprise that all of the major European powers adopted similar tactics.

In 1756, war broke out again, this time between the East India Company and the Nawab of Bengal Despite early successes such as taking Calcutta out of East India Company hands, the Nawab's forces quickly lost ground. In 1757, the East India Company won what has since become known as the crucial Battle of Plassey. This placed Bengal under the East India Company's control; as a prime agricultural area and a province with a population of over 20 million people, this was an enormous coup for the East India Company. The Nawab and his forces continued to fight the British presence in India for several years, at one point forming an allegiance with the Mughal emperor. Despite these efforts, the Nawab and his Mughal allies experienced a resounding defeat at the Battle of Buxar in 1764, and the following year, the Mughal emperor formalized British control of India with the Treaty of Allahabad, which gave the East India Company a kind of provincial governor status over the province of Bengal (Marshall, 492). From this point on, the East India Company officially had the emperor's blessing, which gave their presence in India a new level of legitimacy.

A contemporary depiction of the Nawab of Bengal

Depictions of soldiers at the battle

During the late 18th century, the American War of Independence resulted in the loss of the American colonies. This was more than just a blow to the British ego; the cotton and tobacco produced in the American South were crucial fuel for the Industrial Revolution, which had begun in English textile mills in the previous two decades (Beckles, "Hub of the Empire," 239). In addition, the American colonies had provided an outlet for underemployed or impoverished Britons. In short, the English economy needed new options fast. This facilitated a shifting focus to Asia and Australia as the new center of the British Empire. With the East India Company already in place, this shift proved highly profitable, ultimately leading to a far more powerful phase in British imperial history than they had enjoyed with the North American settler colonies.

While historians typically mark the Battle of Plassey as the start of British rule in India, resistance continued in various forms. Peasant revolts and uprisings, while never successful in driving out the East India Company and their local representatives, occurred with regularity. In 1783, a massive peasant uprising in Rangpur took control of entire regions for over a month, going so far as to elect their own government and replace the old ruler with a new Nawab. East India Company officials brutally suppressed the uprising, which had consisted of men and women from a large cross-section of Rangpur society. At the direction of the East India Company, soldiers put down the revolt by killing civilians without trial. Subsequent peasant revolts erupted throughout the early 19th century. Most of these revolts began as a response to the economic strain of production quotas and tax collection. While some succeeded in inflicting violence and destruction on the East India Company and its local representatives, peasants were never able to form a coalition with which to engage in sustained fighting (Sen, History Modern India, 84-85). Riots and rebellions would erupt, swiftly overtake a region, and then burn out or face opposition once they reached the neighboring province.

Elites continued to engage in more organized military resistance. The most notable of the post-Battle of Plassey figures to challenge East India Company rule was heir to the kingdom of Mysore, Tipu Sultan, who engaged in a series of four wars against East India Company incursions into his kingdom, conflicts collectively known as the Anglo-Mysore Wars. Tipu Sultan was notable for his extensive efforts to assemble an international coalition to oppose British influence in South Asia but despite his best efforts, he was killed in battle in 1799. This is generally considered the last serious attempt to check British expansion across the Indian subcontinent (Roy, War, Culture, and Society, 87).

A depiction of Tipu Sultan

A painting depicting the death of Tipu Sultan at the Battle of Seringapatam in 1799

The Mughal Dynasty, while greatly limited in power and in some ways reduced to symbolic status, officially remained in place until 1858. The dynasty, dating back to 1526, had at one point controlled nearly the entire subcontinent but their power began to decline before they were directly challenged by the East India Company. In the early 18th century they had lost important territories and kingdoms to the Maratha dynasty and other rulers. When the East India Company ascended to power in Bengal, they framed their role as the ally and defender of the Mughal Dynasty, with whom they had long enjoyed good trade relations. In practice, however, this meant that direct Mughal control was only exerted over a very limited area. In addition, they remained largely under the thumb of the East India Company and its strategic needs (Wolpert, New History, 186).

Several late-18th century Governors General made strategic policy choices or major blunders that shaped the political landscape of India. While the first 150 years of East India Company history depended on the entire Court of Directors and a huge number of employees for its policy direction, the centralization of power in the Governor General meant that more and more East India Company policy depended on the decisions of a single individual.

The first of a long line of Indian Governors General was Warren Hastings. By the time he was appointed Governor General in 1773, he had already had a long and eventful career in the Indian Interest. Overseeing such seminal moments as the Battle of Buxar, Hastings developed a reputation as a capable administrator with a relatively open mind about Indian customs and methods of governance. Despite these strengths, he frequently clashed with the Court of Directors in London (Dirks, Scandal of Empire, 394-395).

Hastings

Hastings is perhaps less well-known for his effect on India, however, than he is remembered for his infamous 1788 corruption trial. In Parliament, Charles Fox, a prominent Whig and critic of the East India Company, and his allies sought to limit if not completely dissolve the company. Fox's attempts to pass his India bill depended to a large extent on reports of the wars and punitive actions taken by Hastings during his tenure in India. Edmund Burke was scathing in his critique of the East India Company during debate over Fox's bill:

"These intended rebellions are one of the Company's standing resources. When money has been thought to be heaped up anywhere, its owners are universally accused of rebellion, until they are acquitted of their money and their treasons at once. The money once taken, all accusation, trial, and punishment ends. It is so settled a resource, that I rather wonder how it comes to be omitted in the Directors' account; but I take it for granted this omission will be supplied in their next edition.

"The Company stretched this resource to the full extent when they accused two old women in the remotest corner of India (who could have no possible view or motive to raise disturbances) of being engaged in rebellion, with an intent to drive out the English nation, in whose protection, purchased by money and secured by treaty, rested the sole hope of their existence. But the Company wanted money, and the old women must be guilty of a plot. They were accused of rebellion, and they were convicted of wealth. Twice had great sums been extorted from them, and as often had the British faith guaranteed the remainder. A body of British troops, with one of the military farmers-general at their head, was sent to seize upon the castle in which these helpless women resided. Their chief eunuchs, who were their agents, their guardians, protectors, persons of high rank according to the Eastern manners, and of great trust, were thrown into dungeons, to make them discover their bidden treasures, and there they lie at present. The lands assigned for the maintenance of the women were seized and confiscated. Their jewels and effects were taken, and set up to a pretended auction in an obscure place, and bought at such a price as the gentlemen thought proper to give. No account has ever been transmitted of the articles or produce of this sale. What money was obtained is unknown, or what terms were stipulated for the maintenance of these despoiled and forlorn creatures; for by some particulars it appears as if an engagement of the kind was made. …

"It is only to complete the view I proposed of the conduct of the Company with regard to the dependent provinces, that I shall say any thing at all of the Carnatic, which is the scene, if possible, of greater disorder than the northern provinces. Perhaps it were better to say of this centre and metropolis of abuse, whence all the rest in India and in England diverge, from whence they are fed and methodized, what was said of Carthage, 'De Carthagine satius est silere quam parum dicere.' This country, in all its denominations, is about 46,000 square miles. It may be affirmed, universally, that not one person of substance or property, landed, commercial, or moneyed, excepting two or three bankers, who are necessary deposits and distributors of the general spoil, is left in all that region. In that country, the moisture, the bounty of Heaven, is given but at a certain season. Before the era of our influence, the industry of man carefully husbanded that gift of God. The Gentoos preserved, with a provident and religious care, the precious deposit of the periodical rain in reservoirs, many of them works of royal grandeur; and from these, as occasion demanded, they fructified the whole country. To maintain these reservoirs, and to keep up an annual advance to the cultivators for seed and cattle, formed a principal object of the piety and policy of the priests and rulers of the Gentoo religion…

"The menial servants of Englishmen, persons (to use the emphatical phrase of a ruined and patient Eastern chief) "whose fathers they would not have set with the dogs of their flock", entered into their patrimonial lands. Mr. Hastings's banian was, after this auction, found possessed of territories yielding a rent of one hundred and forty thousand pounds a year.

"Such an universal proscription, upon any pretence, has few examples. Such a proscription, without even a pretence of delinquency, has none. It stands by itself. It stands as a monument to astonish the imagination, to confound the reason of mankind. I confess to you, when I first came to know this business in its true nature and extent, my surprise did a little suspend my indignation. I was in a manner stupefied by the desperate boldness of a few obscure young men, who, having obtained, by ways which they could not comprehend, a power of which they saw neither the purposes nor the limits, tossed about, subverted, and tore to pieces, as if it were in the gambols of a boyish unluckiness and malice, the most established rights, and the most ancient and revered institutions, of ages and nations."

Eager to illustrate the necessity of reducing East India Company influence in India, Fox called for the impeachment of Hastings to set an example. The charges faced by Hastings included extortion and judicial murder of Indian political opponents. The trial began in the House of Lords shortly after Hastings was recalled from India. By its end, the trial had lasted for years and resulted in a verdict of not guilty for most charges. Historians argue that the need to hold distant colonial officials accountable to Parliament and the Crown was in many ways the result of the American War of Independence; after that loss, the British public felt that too much autonomy in colonial administrators was a dangerous thing, even if they technically represented a private company. The Hastings' trial was thus less about the specific acts committed by the Governor General and more about broader concerns about the East India Company and its role in British foreign affairs (Keay, Scandal of Empire, 419-420).

Fox

The second notable Governor General of India was Charles Cornwallis. After enjoying the dubious honor of signing Britain's surrender at the end of the American War of Independence, Earl Cornwallis became the Governor General of India, serving from 1786 to his death in 1793. Cornwallis began his posting in India at a time when the East India Company had experienced considerable victories such as the Battle of Plassey and the Battle of Buxar, yet had also had their reputation diminished by the tragedy of the Bengal Famine and subsequent peasant uprisings (See Sen). Some areas like Mysore remained independent and defiant. In short, Cornwallis began his tenure at a moment when the East India Company's position remained unstable. Cornwallis's task was to entrench East India Company authority in conquered regions, shut down continuing resistance, and create systems of administration and bureaucracy that would stabilize East India Company governance. On all of these counts, Cornwallis is considered a resounding success (Wickwire, Cornwallis, 56-57). The administrative systems created by Cornwallis to replace outdated company policies created the model that would be employed by later East India Company administrators as well as by the British Raj. First, Cornwallis reformed the taxation system to be profitable but not so extreme as to lead to peasant starvation. Second, he altered the way that local Indian employees were selected and paid so that they received higher wages but could not engage in trade with any other enterprise. Militarily, Cornwallis engaged in campaigns against Tipu Sultan and took significant territories (Wickwire, 264-265).

Cornwallis

The third notable Governor General of India responsible for the growth of the East India Company as an imperial power was the Marquess of Wellesley. Wellesley picked up where Cornwallis left off, aiming to subdue any remaining resistance in East India Company-controlled parts of India. In Mysore, Wellesley succeeded where Cornwallis had fallen short, engaging in the campaign that would result in Tipu Sultan's death in 1799. During Wellesley's tenure, the allegiances of Indian rulers took on greater significance as the Napoleonic Wars engulfed much of the world. At this point, only one major Indian kingdom, Maratha, remained free of British influence; Maratha also happened to be a French ally. Wellesley thus spearheaded a campaign against Maratha, emerging victorious in 1803. With this victory, the French presence in India came to an end and the East India Company had no serious rivals for political control in the subcontinent (Bayly, "Wellesley, Richard."). Unlike Cornwallis, Wellesley did not die in India; he went on to hold a number of other government positions including Lord Lieutenant of Ireland (Bayly).

Wellesley

Beginning in 1770, a devastating famine killed as many as 10 million people in the provinces of Bengal and Bihar. While crop shortages and poor harvests were naturally occurring due to poor rainfall that year, the famine itself was not. The famine instead resulted from East India Company policy, which required the growth of inedible cash crops like opium and cotton rather than the food crops that had sustained the population. The famine was further exacerbated by taxation and policies regarding grains, which placed the price of food beyond the reach of peasants (Damodaran, "Famine," 146-148).

The loss of roughly a third of the population in some areas disrupted the economy for decades or even centuries to come. Previously settled agricultural areas became completely depopulated. In addition, some survivors turned to banditry and other forms of crime out of desperation, which increased violence and unrest amongst the peasantry (See Guha, Elementary). The famine also had a negative effect on the company. The millions of famine-related deaths depleted the company's workforce and dramatically reduced the crops harvested in the following years. British public opinion also began to turn against the East India Company as a result of the crisis.

Aside from humanitarian concerns for starving and displaced Bengalis and Biharis, wealthier members of the British public also resented the damage to the company's stock. From 1770, the East India Company went from one of the most outrageously profitable enterprises on the planet to a company that struggled financially, at some points threatened with insolvency (Keay, *Honourable,* 320-323).

Officially, the East India Company controlled India until 1858. In practice, however, the British Crown became increasingly involved from 1770 on, largely due to the tragedy of the famine. The office of Governor General was created to oversee British activities in India, and the British government became more involved in regulating the flow of profits and goods from the colony.

Politics in the Late 18th and Early 19th Centuries

Discussions of the East India Company usually focus on one of two images: the swashbuckling piracy, warfare, and "White Mughal" nabobs of the early years, or the sedate high teas and rounds of croquet of Victorian British India. Between those two moments, however, lies the transitional period of the late 18th and early 19th centuries prior to the official start of the Victorian Period in 1837. This was a period when the East India Company, powerful but bruised by the embarrassment of the Bengal Famine, began to renegotiate its relationship with British officials, and a period when the East India Company began to decline and lose authority from its peak in the 1750s.

The year 1773 marked the beginning of East India Company regulation at the hands of the British Crown. The impetus for this regulation was the Bengal Famine and the subsequent financial crisis of the East India Company. In order to remain solvent, the East India Company required an emergency loan from the Crown. Representatives of the Crown agreed, but used the opportunity to pass the Regulating Act, which asserted British sovereignty over East India Company territories, created the office of the Governor General, and imposed a number of financial regulations on the East India Company's accounting practices in order to ensure transparency. While the East India Company lobby fought the bill in Parliament, the company's financial straits ultimately forced them to agree (Sankey, "Tea Act")

This year also proved crucial to the future of the East India Company and the British Empire for another reason, the Tea Act. The Tea Act altered the duties on Indian tea to make their prices competitive with smuggled Dutch tea, for the purposes of selling to American colonists in order to increase East India Company profits in their time of fiscal crisis. Despite the fact that the Tea Act did not significantly alter the price of tea in the colonies, Americans resented the duties paid on the tea and used the Act as a way of agitating for political change. This famously culminated in the Boston Tea Party and, eventually, the American Revolution. The East India Company thus played an important part in the formation of the United States and the loss of the American colonies (Sankey, "Tea Act").

By the 1780s, the East India Company had gained vast wealth and territory for the British Empire at the same moment that the Crown had lost its most important North American colonies; as a result, the East India Company stood as the single most important component of the British Empire. This is not to suggest, however, that all was well between the East India Company, Parliament, and the British public. On the contrary, late-18th century Britons had significant concerns about the shift in the East India Company's goals and viewed the East India Company as a highly corrupt institution (Philips, The East India Company, 23). The fact that the East India Company had achieved a trade monopoly in India was a source of consternation for free trade supporters. In the two years leading up to the passage of Pitt's India Act, the East India Company and its corruption became the focus of scathing debates within Parliament, which at that time was in a moment of crisis.

Opposition Whig leader Charles Fox took up the regulation of the East India Company as a major cause, which placed him in direct conflict not only with Prime Minister William Pitt but with King George III. Fox's proposed India Bill would have replaced the near-total authority of the Court of Directors with a Parliament-appointed commission that would oversee all East India Company activities. The proposed list of commissioners consisted entirely of Fox's allies, all of whom were vocal critics of East India Company policies. The suggested measures in the bill caused shock and outrage; Pitt used the opportunity to draft his far more moderate bill, which the East India Company was prepared to accept out of fears that Fox's bill would pass instead if they tried to avoid any reform at all. Thus Pitt's India Act of 1784 passed both houses (Philips, 23-24).

William Pitt the Younger

By 1784, the East India Company's Court of Directors and its various committees exercised enough power over the economy and international affairs to be considered a rival to the formal authority of the British state. The Secret Committee was particularly powerful, engaging in diplomacy and warfare without needing to consult representatives of the Crown. They did, however, sometimes collaborate with the British government; the Secretary of State, for example, used the Secret Committee to conduct secret negotiations in India (Philips, 10). Prime Minister William Pitt formally codified this diplomatic power in 1784 with the India Act, which specified the exact nature of the relationship between the Secret Committee and the British government. Pitt rejected suggestions that would have tempered the power of the Court of Directors; the involvement of the British Crown in the 1780s consisted largely of civil service appointments to bureaucratic positions in India (Philips, 11-14). The ambiguities remaining in the Act were clarified two years later with the Act of 1786, which explicitly outlined the relationship between the East India Company and the British Crown (Philips, 60).

The need to have the company's charter periodically renewed gave the East India Company's opponents opportunities to press for changes to the company's structure and practices. While there had been minor changes made to the charter during renewal periods over the years, the first significant and controversial shift occurred in 1813. At this point, the East India Company held a monopoly on trade in Asia, including British trade entrepots in China. This had been the subject of resentment and anger among non-East India Company merchants who found their overseas efforts limited to other parts of the world. During the 17th and 18th centuries, however, opportunities in North America and the Caribbean had remained ample and the Asian trade risky enough that attempts to break up the monopoly had failed to gain sufficient support. By 1813, however, the American colonies had been lost, the slave trade had been abolished, and constant warfare with France had weakened the economy and reduced opportunities for mercantile expansion. The East India Company's monopoly on trade with Asia therefore became far more contentious than in previous years.

However, the East India Company still wielded immense power in Parliament, so independent merchants thus needed a way to sway public opinion to their side. Beginning in 1812, a pamphlet war erupted between free trade advocates and East India Company monopoly supporters. Members of Parliament took sides in the debate, with the powerful and respected Lord Buckinghamshire taking the position that the East India Company monopoly should be forcibly ended. The Court of Directors divided into bickering opposing camps, with some seeking compromise and others who vowed to give no ground on the charter (Philips, 183-186).

While the fight over the East India Company monopoly initially involved only trade-related interests, other groups soon joined in the fight. Most notably, Evangelical Christians who wished to dispatch missionaries to India resented East India Company restrictions on missionary activity in Asia. By siding with independent traders, they hoped to also include changes to the charter specifically permitting Christian proselytizing in East India Company-controlled areas. This aspect of the campaign gained traction when William Wilberforce, famous for his successful efforts to ban the transatlantic slave trade, lent his support.

Wilberforce

As a result, the renewal of the East India Company charter went from an obscure trade issue to the Regency-era equivalent of a media circus, with pamphleteers furiously advancing their position, countless witnesses testifying before the House of Commons, and Christian churches jumping into the fray. In the end, the new charter preserved the East India Company monopoly with China but ended it everywhere else. It also imposed new financial regulations on the company, specified that East India Company territories were ultimately territories of the British Crown, and permitted missionaries to proselytize and build new facilities in India (Philips, 190-193).

This represented a major shift in the East India Company's position; while still nominally the ruling authority over most of India, the East India Company now answered to Parliament and the British Crown. The Charter Act of 1813 also signaled a significant change in how Britons conceptualized their empire and the relationship between themselves and their subjects. With the arrival of missionaries in India, the relationship between colonizer and colonized went beyond harvesting of resources, now encompassing the "civilizing mission" that would eventually develop into the ideology of the White Man's Burden. Missionaries would attempt to bring not only Christianity but also major cultural changes that in some cases had devastating consequences for local economies and kinship systems (See Burton, "White Women's Burden").

The period between 1830 and 1834 has been described by one notable historian as "the company's surrender" (Philips, 276). During this period, the India Interest tried and failed to regain the privileges lost in Pitt's India Act and the Charter Acts. In fact, the company not only failed to regain their privileges, they lost most of what remained. Prominent members of Parliament and the British public had once again called attention to the abuses of the East India Company, which had not been curbed by past legislation. In particular, the case of two Indian bankers unfairly treated by the East India Company gained attention in the British press (Philips, 283).

More than anything else, however, the East India Company was threatened by the Reform Bill, a piece of legislation designed to eliminate "pocket" and "rotten" boroughs from Parliament; these were boroughs that sent a representative to the House of Lords, but that contained few if any residents and thus did not truly warrant representation. Several of the seats eliminated by the Reform Bill were occupied by East India Company Directors, which meant that much of their lobbying power vanished with their seats.

As a result of these changes, Parliament passed the first of what would eventually be several Government of India Acts in 1833. For all practical purposes, the Act ended the East India Company's status as a commercial actor and instead made it a kind of paid administrative body for India. Profits still flowed from India and the East India Company continued to exist as a company, but its purpose had changed. Ruling India, which it had done with such tragic results, now became its central task.

Beyond eliminating the East India Company's commercial status, the Act also centralized power in the office of the Governor General, increased the power of the Board of Control, and created a set of regulations for the implementation of new laws in India. Subsequent Government of India Acts would strip still more power and autonomy from the East India Company and shift authority to Parliament and the Crown (Philips, 288-291).

It is important to remember that the East India Company did not directly administer most of their Indian territories, nor did they typically govern through brute force. Rather, they worked by cultivating relationships with local nobles and merchants, rewarding those who cooperated and working to overthrow those who did not. Mughal Emperor Shah Alam was allowed to remain on the throne in exchange for annual tributes to the East India Company. Bengali elites received part of the profits derived from the sale of cash crops farmed on their lands. Other rulers and elites tacitly cooperated due to fear that failure to do so would result in loss of territory. In this way, the East India Company tapped into the existing system of nobility that allowed Mughal nobility to rule over the vast population of the subcontinent. The East India Company did not have a direct presence in every part of India; rather, they built garrisons and sought to control nobles in strategic locations that gave them de facto control (See Marshall). As a result of this need to constantly cultivate relationships with Indian elites, East India Company representatives existed in a state of tension between the need to enforce separatism and British superiority and the practical need to adopt certain aspects of Indian culture and lifestyle. The level of integration versus separatism favored by the East India Company changed depending on the time period and context.

An 18th century depiction of Shah Alam

Nabob is a term for 18th century Britons who adopted various aspects of Mughal lifestyle during their stay in India. This included clothing, diet, and housing based on the way Mughal nobles lived, and in many cases, nabobs took Indian cultural practices back to Europe when they finished their tour of duty with the East India Company or another Asian venture. The lifestyles adopted by nabobs were completely acceptable in India, but they were the source of frequent controversy upon their return home to Britain. Given their wealth and prestige, adopting a Mughal lifestyle while in India enjoyed tacit acceptance, but this would change in the 19th century when British men serving in India were discouraged from adopting any aspect of Indian culture (Nechtman, Nabobs, 20).

The sexual and social practices of East India Company officials and enlisted men changed immensely from the company's foundation in 1600 to its end in the 19th century. Prior to the mid-19th century, it was highly unusual for East India Company employees to bring wives or children with them during their stay in India. Even after that policy changed, only relatively high-ranking employees could do so. Lower-level employees such as enlisted soldiers could not bring wives with them and the company preferred to recruit men who were not married at all (Levine, Prostitution). During the 18th century, when visiting Europeans sometimes chose to adopt the nabob lifestyle, it was extremely common for them to form permanent or semi-permanent relationships with Indian women. While these rarely resulted in formal marriage, a large percentage of East India Company sailors and other employees listed their Indian concubines and children as the recipients of their salary should they die during a voyage (Dalrymple, White Mughals, 29).

During the Victorian Era, officers and colonial administrators worked to replicate British culture and social life during their stay in India. Unlike the nabobs of the 17th and 18th centuries, who had copied the Mughals on everything from food to architecture, 19th century East India Company officials and representatives of the British state took care to transplant as much of British art, architecture, and fashion as they could. There was a huge emphasis on dinner parties, wearing proper British clothing, and maintaining middle-class respectability. Some aspects of Indian culture such as food were adopted, but in general cultural mixing was frowned upon. This is not to suggest, however, that East India Company employees managed to remain entirely separate from Indian society. Most of the servants in colonial houses were Indian, with one house in the 1820s or 1830s easily having as many as 57 servants (although that number grew smaller in later years). This was the main area in which British men and women interacted with Indians. The British lived mainly in colonial enclaves specifically designed and set aside for British people, rather than among Indians. This formed a striking contrast with the nabobs of the 18th century, who had intermingled with local peoples to a far greater extent.

In the 19th century, it became more common for the wives of high-ranking East India Company officers to accompany their husbands to India. These were middle-class or aristocratic women, permitted to live only in very sheltered environments in British enclaves in various

Indian cities. Popular memory has often blamed British wives for worsening race relations in the colonies because women had a reputation for being more racist, more conservative, and more invested in maintaining British culture even when it was not suitable to the climate or surroundings (such as wool clothing in the Calcutta summer) than their men were. While there is some truth to the idea that women sought to maintain British culture in the colonies, this was a very deliberate strategy on the part of the East India Company and later the administration of the British Raj. They specifically allowed officers to bring their wives because they feared people "going native." Since they saw women as a civilizing influence, women were made to understand that they had that role (Stoler, Carnal Knowledge, 130).

Children born in India typically stayed there for the first few years of their life, often cared for by Indian nannies and learning the local language. By the time they reached school age, however, they would be shipped off to a boarding school or would return to England with one or both of their parents. This was a deliberate strategy to avoid letting British children become too familiar with Indian culture (Stoler, 120). While this strategy successfully maintained ideologies of white supremacy, India remained strikingly present in literature written by people who spent part of their childhood there; authors like Rudyard Kipling, for example, included significant references to India in his poems and fiction.

The rules against mixing with locals did not prevent relationships between British men and Indian women. Many men formed sexual relationships that often produced children. Unlike in earlier centuries, however, these children were often not officially acknowledged by their fathers and the relationships that produced them were not formalized through marriage. The 19th century was a time when scientific racism grew tremendously, which meant that official policy discouraged these relationships whenever possible.

East India Company administrators also had to contend with the cultural effects of another type of undesirable sexual character, the European prostitute. Once British concepts of eugenics and scientific racism began to instill serious fears of miscegenation into the British public and East India Company employees, the practice of British men visiting Indian prostitutes could no longer be tolerated. At the same time, however, the image of the British as morally superior could be seriously damaged by allowing their Indian subjects to see British women working as prostitutes. The solution was to tacitly allow non-British European women, such as Italians and Russians, to travel to India and work in European-only brothels there. This proved immensely profitable, with many of the women working in Bombay brothels able to retire after three years. This outlook on race and prostitution began under the East India Company and became even more prevalent during the British Raj. As this example indicates, the effects of the East India Company and its interactions with Indians had ideological and social implications extending well beyond India or Britain, eventually involving people from the rest of Europe (Tambe, "Elusive Ingénue," 161).

The East India Company in China and Southeast Asia

While no other area under control of the East India Company ever came close to the profits generated by their Indian territories, the East India Company also had ventures in Southeast Asia during the 19th century. The outposts developed in Singapore, Malaysia, and Burma would all become economically and militarily significant to the development of the British Empire. In all of the examples discussed below, colonial outposts began as East India Company projects before passing to the control of the British Crown. In some cases, such as Burma, this meant that the British Crown inherited unstable systems and highly resistant populations, resulting in bloody military intervention.

Despite the profits generated by Indian factories during the 18th century, the East India Company never quite abandoned their quest to establish greater trade ties and acquire territory farther east. While the VOC had long since been surpassed by the East India Company, they remained dominant in the spice islands of Southeast Asia. After several unsuccessful attempts to secure territories in the area, Sir Thomas Stamford Raffles finally secured a trade entrepot with the founding of Singapore in 1819. Consisting of a tiny piece of land and largely unoccupied before East India Company arrival, Singapore nevertheless quickly grew into a crucial trading post, creating the foundation for the major economic power that it has become today (Keay, Honourable Company, 448-449).

Raffles

In 1824, the Anglo-Dutch Treaty granted a large section of former Dutch territory in Southeast Asia to the British. This gave the East India Company permission to establish settlements in formerly contested areas. The three most significant sites were Penang, Melaka, and Dinding. These three sites along with Singapore collectively became known as the Straits Settlements. The Straits Settlements occupied positions of strategic importance, but they were comparatively unprofitable and difficult to manage, largely because they lacked Bengal's existing indigenous population and had to be supplied with migrant workers. The East India Company's presence in these settlements permanently altered the development and demography of the area, creating cities where none had existed before and bringing Chinese and Indian workers to largely Malay-speaking parts of Asia (Turnbull, Straits Settlements, 7).

Burma proved to be a challenge, first for the East India Company and later for the British Crown. In the early 19th century, Burma was ruled by the powerful Konbaung Dynasty and conflicts with the Burmese emerged over the border territories of Northern India. The first of three Anglo-Burmese Wars was an exceedingly costly and difficult war, lasting from 1824 to 1826. It resulted in an East India Company victory and trade and territory concessions on the part of the Burmese. Burma continued to resist British control, however, and it would never be fully pacified during the East India Company's tenure (Aung, History of Burma, 210-265).

China was never officially colonized by a foreign power, but it was forced into a state of economic dependence and informal empire by the East India Company. This included the forcible opening of trading enclaves in certain Chinese ports, most favored nation economic status, and the establishment of neighborhoods occupied entirely by European businessmen and their families. The Opium Wars were a huge factor in this dependent status. The opium trade increased in significance during the early 19th century largely due to increasing demands for Chinese tea and ceramics, combined with the fact that opium was the only British commodity that could turn a significant profit in Chinese markets (Lovell, Opium War, 23-24). Chinese tea achieved particular economic importance in the 18th century as tea drinking became an established feature of British life; imports went from 100 pounds in 1664 to nearly five million pounds in 1750 (Timeline). The Chinese tea trade became even more important during the financial downturn caused by the Bengal Famine. When the East India Company's monopoly was forcibly ended in 1834, they found themselves in competition with other British opium merchants as well as Americans and people of other nationalities who sought a foothold in the trade. Competition exploded, opium prices dropped, and opium became an item of crucial importance for securing sufficient quantities of silk, tea, and ceramics (Philips, 287-288).

During the 19th century, the East India Company began producing cheap opium in large quantities, which they sold to Chinese customers. Opium smoking in China reached epidemic levels, with as much as 90% of the male population using it. In response, the Chinese government outlawed the trade in opium, but the British continued to defy anti-opium laws, and in 1839 numerous British merchants were arrested as a result. War broke out in 1839, at which point it became clear that the Chinese navy was outdated and ill-equipped. British forces quickly won and secured free trade concessions, most favored nation status, and extraterritoriality, which basically meant that British subjects operating in China would not be subject to Chinese law.

The Second Opium War broke out in 1857 over enforcement of the laws of extraterritoriality. Britain, this time acting solely as an imperial state rather than in support of the East India Company, won this war as well, and this time the British secured the opening of all Chinese ports and demands that foreigners be allowed to proselytize on Chinese soil without interference. Several years later, this resulted in the Taiping Rebellion, one of the most destructive conflicts in modern history. In addition, the trade demands placed on Chinese ports led to economic hardship and political repression that would eventually provide backing for the Chinese Communist movements of the late 19th and early 20th centuries (Lovell, 246-247).

The East India Company's Effect on British Culture

Pictures of coins issued by the East India Company

Imperialism was not something that just happened in the colonies; it also affected every aspect of life in Britain. The resources and labor harvested through colonialism shaped industry and economic life. The need for soldiers and personnel created an entire group of people who lived in the colonies for extended periods of time before returning to Britain with new habits, tastes, and ideas. Perhaps most importantly, the interaction between the British and colonized peoples led to major cultural changes and new schools of thought, the most dangerous of which was eugenics.

On a less harmful level, British diet and décor both changed during the 19th century. The British began to eat modified versions of common Indian food like kedgeree and curried rice dishes. Chicken tikka masala, not actually an authentic Indian dish, was invented for British travelers who had returned to Britain but missed Indian cuisine. Tea, coffee, sugar, and tobacco all became more affordable over the course of the century, with tea especially becoming a huge part of British cultural life. Faux-Indian and Chinese artwork also became a common feature of middle-class Victorian homes (Chaudhuri, "Shawls," 232-233). In short, the most quintessentially "English" aspects of culture and society in the British Isles owed a huge debt to Asian practices.

Banking increased due to the influx of capital from East India Company holdings, which strengthened the power of the middle classes. The British aristocracy and gentry also saw the importance of this trend and became involved in investments and the boards of banks. This was a major contributing factor in the ongoing process of British industrialization. Thanks to profits from the colonies, the middle classes became increasingly in control of the British economy. They invested the profits of colonial ventures into new factories and businesses, which in turn stimulated demand for urban industrial workers. During the 19th century, the cultural and economic distance between these classes of people increased immensely, with industrial workers and middle class people participating in totally different economic and social activities. Artisans and working-class Britons attempted in the early years of the East India Company to curb their influence, going so far as to violently attack the East India House in 1667 (Timeline). Their efforts failed, however, and skilled British weavers were soon displaced and forced into factory labor by plentiful Indian textile imports. The profits from these ventures were not, however, evenly distributed, with the standard of living dropping among the urban working classes at the same rate that it rose among merchants and other members of the middle classes.

When East India Company employees and officials returned from their travels in India, they came back with stories of "exotic" natives and barbaric practices. They were thus instrumental in the development of ideologies of British supremacy and racist conceptions of non-Europeans. The East India Company was certainly not the only factor in the development of racism; the transatlantic slave trade, which long predated the East India Company's heyday in India, had already contributed to the formation of white supremacist beliefs in Britain and Western Europe (Fields, "Slavery"). Misleading representations of Indians, however, contributed to the growing belief in clearly divided Western and Eastern civilizations, which of course were viewed as binary opposites. Britons saw themselves as industrious, reserved, and calm, while Asians were constructed as oversexed, indolent, and hedonistic (Said, 36). This Orientalist racial ideology undergirded British imperial expansion and policies applied toward colonized peoples. In addition, the tendency to view Easterners and Westerners as fundamentally incompatible opposites has lingering effects to this day.

The East India Company brought attention to several practices and issues that became emblematic of Indian depravity. After consolidating power in Bengal and other areas under their control, one of the East India Company's policy changes involved the introduction of British courts to replace Hindu jurisprudence. This was framed as replacing the superstition and outdated views of religious courts with the rationality of the British legal system (Wickwire, 74-75).

In addition, both Hinduism and Islam were represented to the British public in a way that emphasized lurid elements like the importance of sexuality in Hindu mysticism. The Kama Sutra, a Hindu text on sexuality, was translated and consumed as pornography in Europe (Sigel, Governing Pleasures, 65-68). This voyeuristic focus on sexuality and other less familiar aspects of Hinduism and Islam allowed Christian missionaries to adopt a civilizing narrative to justify their activities in India (Wolpert, 207-208). Narratives of humanitarianism, of course, deflected attention from the economic and territorial motives of the East India Company and the Crown.

Beyond devaluing the culture of colonized peoples, the East India Company played a part in the 19th-century formation of eugenics and scientific racism. European scientific racism relied heavily on descriptions of the inherent biological "nature" of various non-white peoples. Those with experience in India claimed that Indians had certain inherent characteristics such as high sex drive and lack of motivation. As Lord Thomas Babington Macaulay put it in the mid-19th century, "Against misgovernment such as then afflicted Bengal it was impossible to struggle. The superior intelligence and energy of the dominant class made their power irresistible. A war of Bengalees against Englishmen was like a war of sheep against wolves, of men against demons. The only protection which the conquered could find was in the moderation, the clemency, the enlarged policy of the conquerors. That protection, at a later period, they found. But at first English power came among them unaccompanied by English morality. There was an interval between the time at which they became our subjects and the time at which we began to reflect that we were bound to discharge towards them the duties of rulers. During that interval the business of a servant of the Company was simply to wring out of the natives a hundred or two hundred thousand pounds as speedily as possible, that he might return home before his constitution had suffered from the heat, to marry a peer's daughter, to buy rotten boroughs in Cornwall, and to give balls in St. James's Square."

These stereotypes about the nature of Asians (as well as Africans and indigenous Americans in other parts of the Empire) led to the creation of elaborate biological, racial hierarchies placing Britons at the top and non-Europeans farther down the scale. The development of scientific racism may not have been an intentional goal of the East India Company, but there is no doubt that their longstanding presence in India and Southeast Asia was pivotal in the development of European concepts of racial and cultural hierarchies. These views reinforced British and other European colonialism well after the end of the East India Company, and arguably continue to influence perceptions of race to this day.

The Rebellion of 1857 and the End of the East India Company

By the middle of the 19th century, the East India Company had been losing authority for years, but 1857 marked the end, and the catalyst for its downfall was the Indian Mutiny. The Indian Mutiny, also known as the Sepoy Mutiny or the Rebellion of 1857, was a widespread 1857 uprising against the East India Company that involved people from all levels of Indian society. One of the most important groups was the Indian colonial military, also called sepoys. They became involved due to several factors, including dissatisfaction with their treatment. The immediate cause of the Mutiny, however, was a rumor that the rifle cartridges they used were greased with a combination of beef and pork fat. This angered both Hindu and Muslim soldiers due to their respective religious dietary restrictions and united them against the East India Company (these cartridges had to be ripped open with the teeth, hence the anger over the idea that they would be coated in a forbidden food substance). There is little evidence that this rumor about the cartridges was true, but it served to enrage the populace. Numerous civilians and British officers were killed during the Mutiny, and exaggerated stories of atrocities committed there shocked Britons, encouraging anti-Indian sentiments there (Chakravarty, Indian Mutiny, 93).

Unlike previous uprisings, which had typically been confined to a specific city or region, the 1857 Mutiny covered large swathes of territory. The revolt was centered mainly in the north, involving major cities like Delhi, Lucknow, and parts of the Punjab. Crucially, however, important East India Company areas like Bengal did not join in the rebellion. This meant that the East India Company had enough Indian and British troops to take offensive measures, such as laying siege to rebel-held cities like Lucknow and Delhi (Chakravarty, 135).

Numerous Indian aristocrats also rose up against the East India Company because the East India Company refused to recognize their practices of inheritance. Specifically, the British considered territory up for grabs if there was no legitimate male heir to the throne, while Indian practices allowed adoption and other ways of continuing the royal line. One of the leaders and martyrs of the rebellion was a woman named Rani Lakshmi Bai, who led soldiers into battle and was killed on the battlefield fighting for her adopted son's right to the throne. She has since become a major symbol of Indian nationalism. While Indian independence would not come for almost a century, much of the rhetoric and political organization of groups advocating for independence had its roots in the events of the Mutiny (Singh, Rani, 2).

Rani Lakshmi Bai

The Indian Mutiny ended in 1858 when British forces took the rebel-held city of Gwalior. The East India Company and British Crown forces took retaliatory methods against the rebels, publicly executing many and killing civilians suspected of being rebel sympathizers. The colonial administrations of territories outside of India, such as Burma and Singapore, took preventative measures such as curfews out of fear that the Indian Mutiny would spark similar uprisings across the Empire (Turnbull, 49-50).

The disaster of the Indian Mutiny convinced many that the East India Company was not fit to control India. East India Company policies such as poor pay and treatment of soldiers, combined with their miscalculations regarding the treatment of elites, seemed like transparent and obvious mistakes in the aftermath of the Mutiny. The British Crown assumed control of Indian affairs that year, replacing East India Company officials with government-appointed personnel. Other East India Company holdings, such as the Straits Settlements, had already been placed under the control of the Crown. Formally, the East India Company continued to exist for another fifteen years, although in practice the end came with the Mutiny. In 1873, the East India Company was formally dissolved by an act of Parliament (Wolpert, 236).

Since the East India Company had been gradually losing ground to the British Crown and had essentially shared power with them for years, it comes as no surprise that the practices and customs established by the East India Company remained in place during the British Raj. Among other things, the policies toward sexuality and miscegenation were extended to representatives of the British Crown. In addition, the bureaucracy and trade systems created by the East India Company were easily appropriated by the British Crown, which meant that profits were not lost during the transition phase. In essence, the Crown inherited a system that had developed over the course of centuries, in which constant trial and error had arrived at a set of workable practices that could then be taken up with minimal difficulty.

The East India Company did not affect imperialist expansion in India alone, as the profits and personnel gained there helped to fuel British expansion in other regions as well, such as Africa. On a more abstract level, the politics of the East India Company introduced for the first time a series of important questions that Western powers still grapple with to this day. The East India Company stands as one of the first examples of a private company that achieved political power on the level of a nation-state. The tensions and ethical questions that emerged from that status remain all too relevant today; in an age of multinational corporations like Google and Walmart, which have economies larger than that of many countries, it is only natural to reflect on past examples like the East India Company in which private companies were granted the power of life and death over millions.

Given that, no exploration of British history could hope to arrive at informed conclusions without taking the East India Company into account. The East India Company was not just an economic giant, an agent of British imperialism, or a constant force in British politics, but all of these things. It played a decisive role in the industrialization of Britain, the growth of the British Empire, and significant aspects of British culture such as concepts of race and sexual mores. It made a handful of people wealthy while killing millions of others.

Perhaps more than anything else, the East India Company serves as a reminder that economic history is more than just the movement of capital and commodities. It is also the stories of people who are caught up in larger economic and political struggles beyond their control.

Online Resources

Other books about European history by Charles River Editors

Other books about British history by Charles River Editors

Other books about the British East India Company on Amazon

Other books about the Dutch East India Company on Amazon

Bibliography

Dutch East India Company

1.　Celania, Miss. "The Nutmeg Wars." Neatorama. Purch, Inc., 6 Aug. 2012. Web. 7 Nov. 2016.

2.　Briney, Amanda. "The Dutch East India Company." About. About, Inc., n.d. Web. 7 Nov. 2016.

3.　Crump, Thomas. "The Dutch East Indies Company - The First 100 Years." Gresham College. Gresham College, 1 Mar. 2006. Web. 7 Nov. 2016.

4.　Taylor, Bryan. "The Rise And Fall Of The Largest Corporation In History." Business Insider. Business Insider, Inc., 6 Nov. 2013. Web. 7 Nov. 2016.

5.　Beattie, Andrew. "What Was the First Company to Issue Stock?" Investopedia. Investopedia, LLC, n.d. Web. 7 Nov. 2016.

6.　"VOC Ship Batavia." VOC Historical Society. VOC Historical Society, n.d. Web. 7 Nov. 2016.

7.　Prince, Rob. "Dutch East Indies Company (V.O.C) Timeline." View from the Left Bank. WordPress, 14 Apr. 2015. Web. 7 Nov. 2016.

8.　Colombo, Jesse. "The Dutch "Tulip Mania" Bubble (aka "Tulipomania")." The Bubble Bubble. WordPress, 15 June 2012. Web. 7 Nov. 2016.

9.　Melissa. "A BRIEF HISTORY OF PEPPER." Today I Found Out. WordPress, 21 Jan. 2014. Web. 7 Nov. 2016.

10.　Carr, K. E. "History of Pepper." Quatr. N.p., Apr. 2016. Web. 7 Nov. 2016.

11.　"HISTORY OF SPICES." McCormick Science Institute. McCormick Science Institute, n.d. Web. 7 Nov. 2016.

12.　Beattie, Andrew. "Initial Public Offering - IPO." Investopedia. Investopedia, LLC, n.d. Web. 7 Nov. 2016.

13.　"The Santa Catarina Incident." History SG. National Library Board of Singapore, n.d. Web. 7 Nov. 2016.

14.　Aguirre, Jon. "The Dutch East India Company (VOC): Indonesian Chapter." Indoneo. Indoneo, Inc., 1 Oct. 2015. Web. 7 Nov. 2016.

15. "The 1603 Naval Battle of Changi." History SG. National Library Board of Singapore, n.d. Web. 7 Nov. 2016.

16. Rajagobal, Navin. "Roots of International Law in 1603 Incident off Changi." The Straits Times. Singapore Press Holdings, Ltd., 23 Feb. 2015. Web. 7 Nov. 2016.

17. "The Earliest Close-up Map of Singapore: De Bry, 1606." History Delocalized. Blogspot, 8 Mar. 2015. Web. 7 Nov. 2016.

18. Mostert, Tristan. "Chain of Command: 'The Shameful Fall of Fort Zeelandia'." VOC Warfare. N.p., n.d. Web. 7 Nov. 2016.

19. Steenbrick, Karel. "Jan Pieterszoon Coen." Academia. Academia, n.d. Web. 7 Nov. 2016.

20. "Kasteel Batavia." Spice Island Blog. WordPress, 3 Feb. 2015. Web. 8 Nov. 2016.

21. Gage, Chris. "Chapter 4 – The End of the Struggle: The Tragedy of Amboyna." Ibiblio. N.p., n.d. Web. 7 Nov. 2016.

22. Tsai, Pai-Chuan, and Chi-Ming Ng. "Taiwan Struggling for Independence: A Historical Perspective." Care Taiwan Association. Care Taiwan Association, n.d. Web. 8 Nov. 2016.

23. "Skipping around the Region." The Unlikely Diplomat. WordPress, 9 Oct. 2016. Web. 8 Nov. 2016.

24. "Dejima." The Samurai Archives. N.p., 3 Jan. 2016. Web. 8 Nov. 2016.

25. "Trinh – Nguyen War." Vietnam Tourism. Vietnam National Administration of Tourism, 2 July 2015. Web. 8 Nov. 2016.

26. Chandler, David. "Murder and Mayhem in Seventeenth Century Cambodia." Reviews in History. School of Advanced Study University of London, Feb. 2010. Web. 8 Nov. 2016.

27. Khan, Sher Banu. "Memorandum of the Chiefs of the Civilian Yacht Den Arent (The Eagle) about the City of Aceh in 1689." Arsip Nasional Republik Indonesia. N.p., n.d. Web. 8 Nov. 2016.

28. "Battle of Colachel & Victory Pillar." Online Kanyakumari. WordPress, 29 Nov. 2015. Web. 8 Nov. 2016.

29. "The 1740 Batavia Massacre." Raffles and the British Invasion of Java. WordPress, 4 Feb. 2013. Web. 8 Nov. 2016.

30. Sidarto, Linawati. "Two Centuries of Slavery on Indonesian Soil." The Jakarta Post.

Niskala Media Tenggara, 5 Oct. 2015. Web. 8 Nov. 2016.

31. "An Empire Founded by War Has to Maintain Itself by War... Charles De Montesquieu." Old Salt Books Blog. WordPress, 6 Dec. 2013. Web. 8 Nov. 2016.

32. "The Forgotten History of the Slave Trade." Expatica. Expatica Communications, Inc., 21 July 2003. Web. 8 Nov. 2016.

33. "Most Valuable Companies in History, Adjusted for Inflation." Yahoo Finance Canada. Morningstar, Inc., 1 Nov. 2012. Web. 8 Nov. 2016.

34. Wermoth, Thomas S., ed. America's First River. N.p.: State U of New York, 2009. Print.

35. Unoki, Ko. Mergers, Acquisitions and Global Empires: Tolerance, Diversity and the Success of M&A. N.p.: Routledge, 2012. Print.

36. Toze, Eobald. The Present State Of Europe. N.p.: Palala, 2015. Print.

37. Rogers, Peter. Resilience & the City: Change, (Dis)Order and Disaster (Design and the Built Environment). N.p.: Routledge, 2012. Print.

38. Lach, Donald F. Asia in the Making of Europe, Volume III: A Century of Advance. Book 1: Trade, Missions, Literature (Asia in the Making of Europe Vol. III). N.p.: U Of Chicago, 1993. Print.

39. Bernstein, William J. A Splendid Exchange: How Trade Shaped the World. N.p.: Grove, 2009. Print.

40. Dash, Mike. Batavia's Graveyard: The True Story of the Mad Heretic Who Led History's Bloodiest Mutiny. N.p.: Broadway, 2003. Print.

41. Clulow, Adam. Statecraft and Spectacle in East Asia: Studies in Taiwan-Japan Relations. N.p.: Routledge, 2013. Print.

42. K, D. The World's Must-See Places: A Look Inside More Than 100 Magnificent Buildings and Monuments. N.p.: DK Eyewitness Travel, 2011. Print.

The British East India Company

Abu-Lughod, Janet Lippman. "The World System in the Thirteenth Century: Dead End or Precursor?" Pages 75-101 in Before European Hegemony: The World System AD 1250-1350. Edited by Janet Abu-Lughod. New York: Oxford University Press, 1991.

Aung, Maung Htin. A History of Burma. New York: Columbia University Press, 1967.

Bayly, C.A. "Wellesley, Richard, Marquess Wellesley (1760-1842)." In *Oxford Dictionary of National Biography.* Oxford: Oxford University Press, 2004. Online Edition.

Beckles, Hilary McD. "The 'Hub of Empire': The Caribbean and Britain in the 17th

Century." Pages 218-240 in *The Origins of Empire: British Overseas Enterprise to the Close*

of the 17th Century: The Oxford History of the British Empire, Vol. 1. Edited by Nicholas Canny. Oxford: Oxford University Press, 1998.

Bentley, Jerry. *Old World Encounters: Cross-Cultural Contacts and Exchanges in Pre-Modern Times.* Oxford: Oxford University Press, 1993.

Blaut, J.M. *The Colonizer's Model of the World: Geographical Diffusionism and Eurocentric History.* New York: The Guilford Press, 1993.

Burton, Antoinette. "The White Woman's Burden: British Feminists and the Indian Woman, 1865-1915." *Women's Studies International Forum* 13, 4 (1990): 295-308.

Chakravarty, Gautam. *The Indian Mutiny and the British Imagination.* Cambridge: Cambridge University Press, 2005.

Chaudhuri, Nupur. "Shawls, Jewelry, Curry, and Rice in Victorian Britain." Pages 231-246 in *Western Women and Imperialism: Complicity and Resistance.* Edited by Nupur Chaudhuri and Margaret Strobel. Bloomington: Indiana University Press, 1992.

Dalrymple, William. *White Mughals: Love and Betrayal in 18th-Century India.* New York: Penguin Books, 2004.

Damodaran, Vinita. "Famine in Bengal: A Comparison of the 1770 Famine in Bengal and the 1897 Famine in Chota Nagpur." *The Medieval History Journal* 10, 1-2 (October 2007): 143-181.

Dirks, Nicholas B. *The Scandal of Empire: India and the Creation of Imperial Britain.* Cambridge: The Belknap Press, 2006.

Dutt, Romesh Chunder. *The Economic History of India Under Early British Rule From the Rise of British Power in 1757 to the Accession of Queen Victoria in 1837,* Volume I, Reprint Edition. London: Routledge, 2001.

Farrington, Anthony. *Trading Places: The East India Company and Asia, 1600-1834.* London: The British Library, 2002.

Fields, Barbara Jeanne. "Slavery, Race, and Ideology in the United States of America." *The New Left Review* 181 (May/June 1990).

Guha, Ranajit. *Elementary Aspects of the Peasant Insurgency in Colonial India.* North Carolina: Duke University Press, 1999.

Hagerman, Chris. "Sepoy." Pages 1005-1007 in *Encyclopedia of Western Colonialism Since 1450.* Edited by Thomas Benjamin. New York: Macmillan Reference, 2006.

Keay, John. *The Honourable Company: A History of the English East India Company.* London: HarperCollins, 1991.

Levine, Philippa. *Prostitution, Race, and Politics: Policing Venereal Disease in the British Empire.* London: Routledge, 2003.

Lovell, Julia. *The Opium War: Drugs, Dreams, and the Making of China.* London: Picador, 2011.

Makepeace, Margaret. *The East India Company's London Workers: Management of the Warehouse Labourers, 1800-1858.* London: Boydell Press, 2010.

Marshall, P.J. ed. *The Oxford History of the British Empire, Volume II: The 18th Century.* Oxford: Oxford University Press, 1998.

Philips, C.H. *The East India Company, 1784-1834.* Manchester: Manchester University Press, 1961.

Roy, Kaushik. *War, Culture, and Society in Early-Modern South Asia, 1740-1849.* London: Routledge, 2013.

Said, Edward. *Orientalism,* Paperback Edition. New York: Vintage Books, 1979.

Sankey, Margaret. "Tea Act of 1773." In *The American Economy: A Historical Encyclopedia.* Edited by Cynthia L. Clark. Santa Barbara: ABC-CLIO, 2011.

Sen, S.N. *History of Modern India 1765-1950,* Second Edition. New Jersey: John Wiley and Sons, 1986.

Sigel, Lisa Z. *Governing Pleasures: Pornography and Social Change in England, 1815-1914.* New Jersey: Rutgers University Press, 2002.

Singh, Harleen. *The Rani of Jhansi: Gender, History, and Fable in India.* Cambridge: Cambridge University Press, 2014.

Spivak, Gayatri Chakravorty. "Can the Subaltern Speak?" Pages 271-387 in *Marxism and the Interpretation of Culture.* Edited by Cary Nelson. Illinois: University of Illinois Press, 1987.

Stein, Barbara and Stanley. *Silver, Trade, and War: Spain and America in the Making of Early-Modern Europe*. Baltimore: Johns Hopkins University Press, 2003.

Stoler, Ann Laura. *Carnal Knowledge and Imperial Power: Race and the Intimate in Colonial Rule*. Berkeley: University of California Press, 2002.

Tambe, Ashwini. "The Elusive Ingénue: A Transnational Feminist Analysis of European Prostitution in Colonial Bombay." *Gender and Society* 19, 2 (April 2005): 160-179.

"Timeline." *The East India Company, London.* Available at http://www.theeastindiacompany.com/.

Turnbull, C.M. *The Straits Settlements, 1826-67: Indian Presidency to Crown Colony*. London: Athlone Press, 1972.

Wickwire, Franklin and Mary. *Cornwallis: The Imperial Years*. Chapel Hill: University of North Carolina Press, 1980.

Wolpert, Stanley, *A New History of India,* Seventh Edition. Oxford: Oxford University Press, 2004.

Free Books by Charles River Editors

We have brand new titles available for free most days of the week. To see which of our titles are currently free, click on this link.

Discounted Books by Charles River Editors

We have titles at a discount price of just 99 cents everyday. To see which of our titles are currently 99 cents, click on this link.

Printed in Great Britain
by Amazon

55831405R00057